Second Workshop on Shortcomings in Vision and Language (SiVL 2019)

Minneapolis, Minnesota, USA
6 June 2019

ISBN: 978-1-5108-8772-5

NAACL HLT 2019

Second Workshop on Shortcomings in Vision and Language (SiVL)

Proceedings of the Workshop

June 6, 2019
Minneapolis, USA

Introduction

Welcome to the second edition of Workshop on Shortcomings in Vision and Language (SiVL) at NAACL. The first installment of SiVL was held at ECCV 2018 (the European Conference on Computer Vision). SiVL's primary purpose is to bring together researchers at the intersection of vision and language to discuss shortcomings of modern approaches, tasks, data-sets, and evaluation metrics. By highlighting common shortcomings in these domains, the workshop aims to facilitate discussion of novel research directions and to steer the community towards high-level challenges affecting the vision and language community broadly. This year, we called both for Full Papers and Extended Abstracts. The Full Papers are published in these proceedings whereas the extended abstracts are available from the workshop website.

The works in these proceedings highlight the following shortcomings of current tasks, data-sets and metrics.

One main important issue concerns the difference between data-sets annotated by subjects on demand versus naturalistic ones. Because of these differences, models trained on the former are not necessarily suitable for the latter. Findings from some of the submitted works call for new and richer data-sets that exhibit semantic and pragmatic diversity as well as new metrics that take these qualitative aspects of the generated data into account.

Another important concern is about bias in visual and language grounding tasks. Works studying the bias problem points at the importance of finding models that can cope with biases, maybe even exploit them when data are aligned with bias, but override them when they are not. Crucially, in-depth evaluation analyses have to be conducted to guarantee the stability of the models' results.

SiVL-2019 received 13 valid full-paper submissions among which 2 were withdrawn before reviewing phase. The remaining papers received a minimum of 3 double-blind reviews from our highly qualified program committee. Among these, we accepted 8 papers to appear in the workshop. We also received 7 extended abstract submissions, all of which were accepted to appear in the workshop based on the topic relevance determined by the organizing committee.

In addition to full papers and extended abstracts, SiVL-2019 program also includes three invited talks by Yoav Artzi, Angeliki Lazaridou and Margaret Mitchell, thanks to our sponsor SAP. SiVL has also received a sponsorship by Google AI Language.

Organizers:

Raffaella Bernardi, University of Trento (Italy)
Raquel Fernandez, University of Amsterdam (Netherlands)
Spandana Gella, Amazon AI (USA)
Kushal Kafle, Rochester Institute of Technology (USA)
Christopher Kanan, Rochester Institute of Technology (USA)
Stefan Lee, Georgia Tech (USA)
Moin Nabi, SAP SE (Germany)

Program Committee:

Aaditya Prakash, Brandeis University
Abhisek Das, Georgia Tech
Aishwarya Agrawal, Georgia Tech
Alane Suhr, Cornell University
Albert Gatt, University of Malta
Anna Rohrbach, University of California, Berkeley
Aurelie Herbelot, University of Trento
Brandon Birmingham, University of Malta
Carina Silberer, Universitat Pompeu Fabra
Damien Teney, The University of Adelaide
David Schlangen, Bielefeld University
Desmond Elliott, University of Copenhagen
Douwe Kiela, Facebook AI Research
Elia Bruni, University of Amsterdam
Emiel van Miltenburg, Tilburg University
Enver Sangineto, University of Trento
Iacer Calixto, University of Amsterdam
Ivan Vulic, University of Cambridge
Jasper Uijlings, Google AI
Justin Johnson, Stanford University
Katerina Pastra, Cognitive Systems Research Institute
Lisa Anne Hendricks, UC Berkeley
Lucia Specia, University of Sheffield
Malihe Alikhani, Rutgers University
Manoj Acharya, Rochester Institute of Technology
Nazli Ikizler-Cinbis, Hacettepe University
Peratham Wiriyathammabhum, University of Maryland, College Park
Pranava Madhyastha, University of Sheffield
Ramakanth Pasunuru, UNC Chapel Hill
Ranjay Krishna, Stanford University
Robik Shreshtha, Rochester Institute of Technology
Sandro Pezzelle, University of Amsterdam
Sina Zarriess, Bielefeld University
Volkan Cirik, Carnegie Mellon University
Yash Goyal, Georgia Tech

Invited Speaker:

Yoav Artzi, Cornell Tech
Angeliki Lazaridou, Deepmind
Margaret Mitchell, Google Research

Table of Contents

Adversarial Regularization for Visual Question Answering: Strengths, Shortcomings, and Side Effects
Gabriel Grand and Yonatan Belinkov 1

Referring to Objects in Videos Using Spatio-Temporal Identifying Descriptions
Peratham Wiriyathammabhum, Abhinav Shrivastava, Vlad Morariu and Larry Davis 14

A Survey on Biomedical Image Captioning
John Pavlopoulos, Vasiliki Kougia and Ion Androutsopoulos 26

Revisiting Visual Grounding
Erik Conser, Kennedy Hahn, Chandler Watson and Melanie Mitchell 37

The Steep Road to Happily Ever after: an Analysis of Current Visual Storytelling Models
Yatri Modi and Natalie Parde 47

"Caption" as a Coherence Relation: Evidence and Implications
Malihe Alikhani and Matthew Stone 58

Learning Multilingual Word Embeddings Using Image-Text Data
Karan Singhal, Karthik Raman and Balder ten Cate 68

Grounded Word Sense Translation
Chiraag Lala, Pranava Madhyastha and Lucia Specia 78

Conference Program

Shortcomings in vision and language (SiVL) is a full-day event with three plenary talks, spotlight talks for accepted full paper submissions and poster presentations for all accepted full papers and extended abstracts. Presenters are welcome to present their posters during both sessions, but at the minimum are expected to be present during their designated session, i.e., session 1 for abstracts and session 2 for full papers.

The full schedule is presented below.

Thursday, June 6, 2019

09:00–09:10   *Welcome and Opening Remarks*

09:10–10:00   *Invited Talk 1: Angeliki Lazaridou*

10:00–11:20   *Poster Session 1: Abstracts (with coffee break 10:30 - 11:00)*

11:20–12:30   *Spotlight Talks (Full Papers)*

12:30–14:10   *Lunch*

14:10–14:50   *Invited Talk 2: Margaret Mitchell*

14:50–16:10   *Poster Session 2: Full Papers (with coffee break 15:30 - 16:00)*

16:10–17:00   *Invited Talk 3: Yoav Artzi*

17:00–17:30   *Closing Remarks and Panel Discussion*

Adversarial Regularization for Visual Question Answering: Strengths, Shortcomings, and Side Effects

Gabriel Grand[1] and **Yonatan Belinkov**[1,2]
[1]Harvard John A. Paulson School of Engineering and Applied Sciences
[2]MIT Computer Science and Artificial Intelligence Laboratory
Cambridge, MA, USA
ggrand@alumni.harvard.edu, belinkov@seas.harvard.edu

Abstract

Visual question answering (VQA) models have been shown to over-rely on linguistic biases in VQA datasets, answering questions "blindly" without considering visual context. Adversarial regularization (AdvReg) aims to address this issue via an adversary sub-network that encourages the main model to learn a bias-free representation of the question. In this work, we investigate the strengths and shortcomings of AdvReg with the goal of better understanding how it affects inference in VQA models. Despite achieving a new state-of-the-art on VQA-CP, we find that AdvReg yields several undesirable side-effects, including unstable gradients and sharply reduced performance on in-domain examples. We demonstrate that gradual introduction of regularization during training helps to alleviate, but not completely solve, these issues. Through error analyses, we observe that AdvReg improves generalization to binary questions, but impairs performance on questions with heterogeneous answer distributions. Qualitatively, we also find that regularized models tend to over-rely on visual features, while ignoring important linguistic cues in the question. Our results suggest that AdvReg requires further refinement before it can be considered a viable bias mitigation technique for VQA.

1   Introduction

In recent years, the Visual Question Answering (VQA) community has grown increasingly cognizant of the confounding role that bias plays in VQA research. Many popular VQA datasets have been shown to contain systematic language biases that enable models to cheat by answering questions "blindly" without considering visual context (Agrawal et al., 2016; Zhang et al., 2016; Goyal et al., 2017; Agrawal et al., 2018).

Efforts to address this problem have mainly focused on constructing more balanced datasets (Zhang et al., 2016; Goyal et al., 2017; Johnson et al., 2017; Chao et al., 2018). However, any benchmark that involves crowdsourced data is likely to encode certain cognitive and/or social biases (van Miltenburg, 2016; Misra et al., 2016; Eickhoff, 2018). An alternate approach is to develop models that can generalize to novel domains with different biases. In this spirit, Agrawal et al. (2018) introduced VQA under Changing Priors (VQA-CP), a new benchmark in which the distribution of answers varies significantly between train and test splits. Existing models, which tend to rely heavily on the distribution of answers in the training set, perform poorly on VQA-CP (Agrawal et al., 2018).

One approach to mitigating bias that has recently gained interest is a technique called adversarial regularization (AdvReg). In AdvReg, an adversary sub-network performs an inference task based on a subset of the input features; in this case, the adversary attempts to predict answers based only on the question. Successful performance by the adversary indicates that the main network has learned a biased input representation. Negated gradient updates from the adversary are backpropagated to a shared encoder to encourage the main network to learn a bias-neutral representation of the question. Recently, Ramakrishnan et al. (2018) applied AdvReg to VQA and found that it improves generalization to out-of-domain examples on VQA-CP test.

Despite this initial success, AdvReg is still a relatively new methodology, and its effects on representation learning in neural networks remain largely unknown. In this study, we explore AdvReg with the goal of better understanding how this technique affects inference in VQA models. We apply AdvReg to the Pythia VQA architec-

1

Proceedings of the Second Workshop on Shortcomings in Vision and Language, pages 1–13
Minneapolis, USA, June 6, 2019. ©2017 Association for Computational Linguistics

ture (Jiang et al., 2018b), achieving a new state-of-the-art on VQA-CP v1 and v2. However, we find that AdvReg yields a number of previously unreported and undesirable side-effects. We first observe that AdvReg introduces significant noise into gradient updates that creates instability during training. This finding motivates the introduction of a new scheduling technique that gradually introduces regularization over the course of training. We find that scheduling improves gradient stability in the early phases of adversarial training and improves performance on VQA-CP v2. However, even with scheduling, AdvReg significantly reduces performance on in-domain examples. This side-effect suggests that like many statistical regularization methods, AdvReg offers a trade-off between in-domain and out-of-domain performance.

To investigate the strengths and weaknesses of regularized models, we perform quantitative and qualitative error analyses. We find that AdvReg is especially helpful with Yes/No questions, but reduces performance on questions with heterogeneous answers. We also visualize a number of successes and failures of AdvReg, revealing that regularized models often ignore linguistic cues in the question and are heavily swayed by salient visual features. These findings suggest an under-utilization of key information in the question.

The contributions of this work are two-fold. First, we share practical tips for dealing with the idiosyncrasies of AdvReg. Second, we highlight some core drawbacks of AdvReg that have not previously been reported in the literature. By drawing attention to these shortcomings, we hope to motivate future efforts to refine AdvReg.

2 Related Work

Biases in VQA datasets A growing body of work points to the existence of biases in popular VQA datasets (Agrawal et al., 2016; Zhang et al., 2016; Jabri et al., 2016; Goyal et al., 2017; Johnson et al., 2017; Chao et al., 2018; Agrawal et al., 2018; Thomason et al., 2018). In VQA v1 (Antol et al., 2015), for instance, for questions of the form, "What sport is...?", the correct answer is "tennis" 41% of the time, and for questions beginning with "Do you see a...?" the correct answer is"yes" 87% of the time (Zhang et al., 2016). By exploiting these biases, models can disregard the image and still achieve high VQA scores.

Biases in other language tasks Language biases have also been reported in natural language inference (NLI) (Gururangan et al., 2018; Tsuchiya, 2018; Poliak et al., 2018), reading comprehension (Kaushik and Lipton, 2018), and story cloze completion (Schwartz et al., 2017). Many of these tasks are concerned with inferring the relationship between two objects. As in VQA, models can often succeed by learning biases associated with one of these objects, while ignoring the other.

Biases in other vision tasks Images can also encode certain associative biases. For instance, the Commmon Objects in Context (COCO) image dataset (Lin et al., 2014), which is used in VQA, has been shown to contain prominent gender biases (Zhao et al., 2017; Hendricks et al., 2018). Recently, Hendricks et al. (2018) introduced a technique that encourages the assignment of equal gender probability when gender information is occluded from an image. Their Appearance Confusion Loss can be viewed as a vision captioning analogue to AdvReg for VQA.

Mitigating bias Initial efforts to address bias in VQA focused on debiasing existing datasets. VQA v2 introduced complimentary examples with different answers to every question (Goyal et al., 2017). While VQA v2 resulted in a near 50/50 balance for Yes/No questions, the distribution for non-binary questions (e.g., "What type of...?"; "What sport is...?") remains skewed towards a handful of top answers (Goyal et al., 2017).

Given the difficulty of isolating bias from crowdsourced data, researchers have instead begun to emphasize generalization to new domains with different biases. In this line, Agrawal et al. (2018) introduced VQA-CP, a re-division of the existing VQA datasets in which the distribution of answers per question type is inverted between train and test splits. For instance, in the VQA-CP v1 train split, "tennis" is the most frequent answer for the question "What sport is...?", while "skiing" is very uncommon; in the test split, this prior is reversed. Most relevant to our work, Ramakrishnan et al. (2018) applied AdvReg to VQA-CP, and found that it improved test performance over a non-regularized model. Similarly, Belinkov et al. (2019) analyzed the effects of using AdvReg to address bias in NLI. In this work, we analyze the effects of AdvReg on VQA models in further detail, complement AdvReg with a scheduling scheme, and point to remaining limitations in its behavior.

3 Methods

3.1 Adversarial Regularization

Many modern VQA architectures adhere to a common modular design (Jiang et al., 2018b) consisting of the following four components:

- $f_v(I; \theta_v) : I \mapsto v$ Image encoder
- $f_q(Q; \theta_q) : Q \mapsto q$ Question encoder
- $f_z(v, q; \theta_z) : v, q \mapsto z$ Multimodal fusion
- $g_{\text{VQA}}(z; \theta_{\text{VQA}}) : z \mapsto P(a)$ Answer classifier

Composing these components, we obtain the following expression for the base VQA model. This model is trained to minimize cross entropy loss:[1]

$$P(a|I, Q) = g_{\text{VQA}}(f_z(f_v(I), f_q(Q))) \quad (1)$$

$$\mathcal{L}_{\text{VQA}} = -\sum_i a_i \log P(a_i|I, Q) \quad (2)$$

In AdvReg, we introduce an adversarial classifier $g_{\text{ADV}}(q; \theta_{\text{ADV}})$, which attempts to infer the correct answer from only the question features. g_{ADV} shares the same question feature extractor f_q as the base VQA model. However, f_q and g_{ADV} are separated by a gradient reversal layer (GRL). The GRL is a pseudo-function that negates gradients on the backward pass; otherwise, it leaves inputs unchanged:

$$\text{GRL}_\lambda(x) = x \qquad \frac{\partial \text{GRL}_\lambda}{\partial x} = -\lambda_{\text{GRL}} \quad (3)$$

where λ_{GRL} is a hyperparameter. As above, the adversary is trained to minimize the cross entropy loss $\mathcal{L}_{\text{ADV}}$:

$$P(a|Q) = g_{\text{ADV}}(\text{GRL}_\lambda(f_q(Q))) \quad (4)$$

$$\mathcal{L}_{\text{ADV}} = -\sum_i a_i \log P(a_i|Q) \quad (5)$$

The adversarial relationship between the main model and the adversary can be expressed as:

$$\min_{\theta_{v,q,z,\text{VQA}}} \max_{\theta_{q,\text{ADV}}} \mathcal{L} = \mathcal{L}_{\text{VQA}} - \lambda_{\text{ADV}}\mathcal{L}_{\text{ADV}} \quad (6)$$

where the regularization coefficient $\lambda_{\text{ADV}} \geq 0$ controls the trade-off between performance on VQA and robustness to language bias. Additionally, $\lambda_{\text{GRL}} \geq 0$ (from Eq. 3) scales the reversed

---

[1]Since the VQA evaluation metric includes ground truth answers from 10 different subjects, we follow the top-performing models in using a soft target, multi-label variant of the cross entropy objective (see Teney et al. 2018).

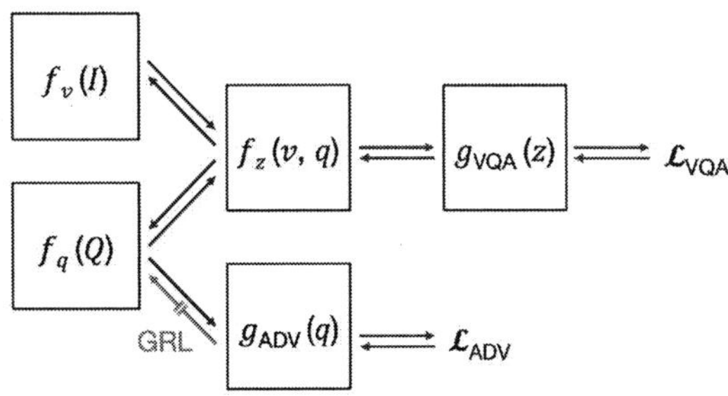

Figure 1: Schematic diagram of adversarial VQA architecture. Right and left arrows represent forward and backward propagation, respectively. The red arrow indicates the gradient reversal layer.

gradients. These two hyperparameters perform related, but different, functions. Setting either or both to zero disables the regularization, since f_q receives no gradients from the adversary. This combination is equivalent to the baseline model. Meanwhile, setting $\lambda_{\text{ADV}} > 0, \lambda_{\text{GRL}} > 0$ enables AdvReg. This setting is the main focus of our experiments.

3.2 Gradient Reversal Layer Scheduling

Because the GRL counteracts the main gradient updates, AdvReg produces noisy gradients that can interfere with learning, as we observe in the experiments below (Fig. 4). To improve stability during the early stages of training, we experiment with a scheduling regime for the gradient reversal layer similar to that used in domain-adversarial neural networks (Ganin et al., 2016). During training, we delay the introduction of regularization for the first μ iterations, which allows f_q to receive clean gradients from the VQA model. Next, we have a warmup phase for w iterations, in which we increase λ_{GRL} linearly from 0 to some constant c:

$$\lambda_{\text{GRL}}(t) = \begin{cases} 0 & t \leq \mu \\ \frac{c(t-\mu)}{w} & \mu \leq t \leq \mu + w \\ c & t > \mu + w \end{cases} \quad (7)$$

GRL scheduling introduces two new hyperparameters, μ and w, which we set by grid search; further details are given in Appendix A.2.

4 Experimental Setup

4.1 Data

We evaluated the performance of our AdvReg setup on VQA-CP v1 and v2 (Agrawal et al., 2018). We also retrained our best-performing models with the same hyperparameter settings on

Model	λ_{ADV}	λ_{GRL}	VQA-CP v1 (test)				VQA-CP v1 (val)				VQA v1 (val)
			Overall	Yes/No	Num.	Other	Overall	Yes/No	Num.	Other	Overall
Baseline	0	0	37.87	42.58	14.16	42.71	**65.79**	86.98	40.06	56.41	**62.68**
+ AdvReg	0.01	0.1	**45.69**	77.64	13.21	26.97	46.94	65.32	32.95	37.22	46.34
+ GRL Sch.	0.01	0.1	44.09	75.01	13.40	25.67	46.45	67.28	29.11	35.71	46.71
			VQA-CP v2 (test)				VQA-CP v2 (val)				VQA v2 (val)
Baseline	0	0	38.80	41.70	12.17	44.59	**67.76**	84.76	49.22	57.04	**63.27**
+ AdvReg	0.005	1	36.33	59.33	14.01	30.41	50.63	67.39	38.81	38.37	48.78
+ GRL Sch.	0.005	1	**42.33**	59.74	14.78	40.76	56.90	69.23	42.50	49.36	51.92

Table 1: Performance comparison of baseline and adversarially-trained models on VQA-CP/VQA v1 and v2 datasets using the best-performing hyperparameters.

VQA v1 (Antol et al., 2015) and v2 (Goyal et al., 2017) in order to evaluate performance on datasets without changing priors.

One difficulty of working with VQA-CP is the lack of validation sets. Ramakrishnan et al. (2018) explain that VQA-CP does not provide validation sets due to the difficulty in varying the answer distributions of binary questions across more than two splits. The authors note that, in place of early stopping, they train their models "until convergence."[2] Although the nonstandard structure of VQA-CP makes validation tricky, we believe it is important to have some mechanism to distinguish between overfitting to language priors and overfitting to the examples in the training set (the latter may occur regardless of the presence of language biases). Our solution is to train models on 90% of the training data and reserve the remaining 10% (sampled randomly) for validation. Score on the val split is useful as an early stopping metric, but does not forecast test performance. In this way, we are able to prevent our models from overfitting to the training data, while remaining agnostic to the distribution of priors in the test set.

While the addition of a VQA-CP val set enables early stopping, models that perform best on the val set will tend to be under-regularized, since AdvReg reduces in-domain performance. We considered creating a second val set derived from VQA-CP test for model selection. However, in addition to introducing additional complexity, this approach would both compromise our ability to remain agnostic to the test set and make our results incomparable with prior work. Therefore, we follow Ramakrishnan et al. (2018) and perform model selection on VQA-CP test. However, to increase transparency, we report results across a broad range of hyperparameters. We hope that recognition of these challenges will motivate the introduction of a standard val set for VQA-CP.

4.2 Implementation

Our experimental setup is based on the Pythia implementation of the Bottom-Up / Top-Down VQA model (Jiang et al., 2018a; Anderson et al., 2018).[3] The adversarial classifier g_{ADV} is implemented as a two-layer fully-connected network with 512 hidden units and ReLU activation. Unless otherwise noted, we use the default hyperparameters from Pythia. Additional details are available in Appendix A.1.

5 Results

5.1 Strengths of AdvReg

Table 1 summarizes the results of the baseline model and the best performing adversarially regularized models. On the VQA-CP v1 test set, our best AdvReg model outperforms the baseline by 7.82%, attaining a new state-of-the-art for this task. On the VQA-CP v2 test set, our best AdvReg model performs worse than the baseline; however, with GRL scheduling, it surpasses the baseline by 3.53%, again setting a new state-of-the-art. Note that in both cases, our models perform better than Ramakrishnan et al. (2018), who report scores of 43.43% and 41.17% on VQA-CP v1 and v2 test, despite the fact that we use only 90% of the available training data. This result indicates that allocating 10% for validation helps prevent overfitting to the training examples.

To highlight how AdvReg mitigates overfitting, Fig. 2 plots loss curves of the baseline (blue)

---

[2]In correspondence, the authors clarified that they trained for a fixed interval determined by the number of iterations to reach peak performance on VQA v2. Since overfitting tends to occur more rapidly on VQA-CP, we view an in-domain val split as a more reliable early stopping metric.

[3]Our code is available at `https://github.com/gabegrand/adversarial-vqa`

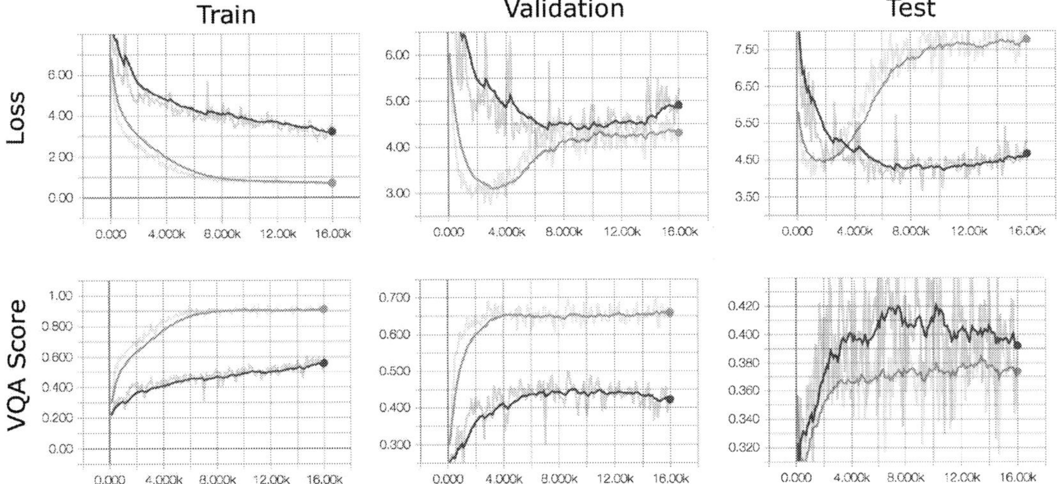

Figure 2: Comparison of regularized (red) and baseline (blue) models on VQA-CP v1 train, val, and test. The baseline model exhibits severe overfitting on both the val and test splits. In contrast, the regularized model overfits much less and achieves a higher score on VQA-CP test.

and regularized (red) models during training. The baseline model exhibits severe overfitting on both VQA-CP v1 val and test. Note that overfitting on the test set appears around 2000 iterations as the model begins to over-rely on language priors. In contrast, overfitting on the val set appears later (around 3500 iterations) as the model begins to memorize the training examples.

In general, AdvReg works well out-of-box on VQA-CP v1. Many of the hyperparameter combinations we tested (Fig. 3) outperform the baseline on VQA-CP v1 test. The key to successful regularization appears to be balancing λ_{ADV} and λ_{GRL}. As Fig. 3 reveals, large values of λ_{ADV} perform better with small values of λ_{GRL}, and vice-versa. However, when λ_{ADV} is too small, AdvReg fails to improve performance; none of the models we tested with $\lambda_{ADV} = 0.001$ outperformed the baseline. On the other hand, when λ_{ADV} is too large, training becomes unstable; for $\lambda_{ADV} > 1$ (not shown), we observed many training runs failing to converge due to exploding gradient values.

5.2 Shortcomings of AdvReg

The improved performance on the out-of-domain test sets comes at the expense of performance on the in-domain validation sets. As Table 1 shows, on both VQA-CP v1 and v2 val, AdvReg models significantly under-performed the baseline (-18.85% and -10.66%, respectively). Retraining with the same hyperparameters on the original VQA v1 and v2 datasets yielded similar results.

Notably, these findings differ from Ramakrishnan et al. (2018), who report only minimal reductions in performance on VQA v1 and v2 from AdvReg. One explanation is that the gains we observed on VQA-CP test relative to Ramakrishnan et al. resulted in diminished performance on VQA-CP val. Indeed, across all runs of our experiments, we found that score on VQA-CP v1 test correlated negatively with score on the val split ($r^2 = -0.355$, $p = 0.013$).[4] In their work, Ramakrishnan et al. also introduce a secondary "difference of entropies" (DoE) regularizer, which they find improves in-domain performance and helps to stabilize adversarial training. However, even without DoE, they report margins of only 1-4% between their AdvReg and baseline models. Ultimately, these unaccounted differences may be due to implementation details, suggesting the need for a closer comparison.[5]

Our results also highlight interesting differences between VQA-CP v1 and v2. On VQA-CP test, the gains due to AdvReg were more significant on v1 as compared to v2. However, on the validation sets, the losses were also greater. This pattern also applied with respect to the original versions of these datasets (i.e., VQA v1 and v2). These findings support the notion that VQA v2 is indeed less biased than v1.

---

[4]We did not find a significant correlation between test and val performance on VQA-CP v2 ($r^2 = 0.237$, $p = 0.141$).

[5]To our knowledge, code from (Ramakrishnan et al., 2018) is not public at present.

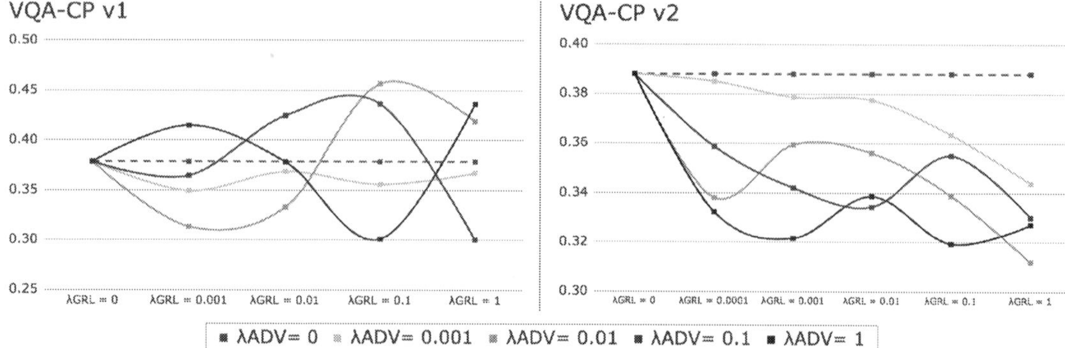

Figure 3: Hyperparameter sweep on VQA-CP v1 and v2 test. Each line is a different setting of λ_{ADV}; lighter/darker red indicates less/more regularization, respectively. λ_{GRL} is varied along the x-axis. Blue dashes: baseline score.

5.3 Effect of GRL scheduling

Without GRL scheduling, none of the AdvReg hyperparameter combinations we tested outperformed the baseline on VQA-CP v2 test (see Fig. 3). This finding may be attributed to the substantial amount of noise that the adversary injects into the gradient updates for the question encoder, as demonstrated by recording gradient norms throughout training.

As Fig. 4 illustrates, on VQA-CP v2, GRL scheduling reduces gradient instability early in training, allowing the model to converge to a lower loss value. In the best-performing schedule, regularization was delayed until $\mu = 2000$ iterations, and slowly warmed up for the following $w = 4000$ steps. This schedule resulted in a 6.00% performance increase on VQA-CP v2 test compared to using the same regularization coefficients without GRL scheduling, and a 3.53% improvement over the baseline (see Table 1).

On VQA-CP v1, we did not observe commensurate improvements from GRL scheduling. We hypothesize that introducing AdvReg on a delay may not be as effective on v1 due to the more prominent biases in this dataset. Note that the baseline model begins to overfit roughly twice as quickly on VQA-CP v1 as on VQA-CP v2 (Fig. 4, Baseline loss). Accordingly, in addition to sweeping the same hyperparameters tested on VQA-CP v2, we experimented with accelerated GRL schedules for VQA-CP v1. While five of the runs outperformed the baseline, three of these were with no start delay. Moreover, all of the runs with GRL scheduling performed worse than a model with the same regularization coefficients with static λ_{GRL}. Finally, many of the runs on VQA-CP v1, and es-

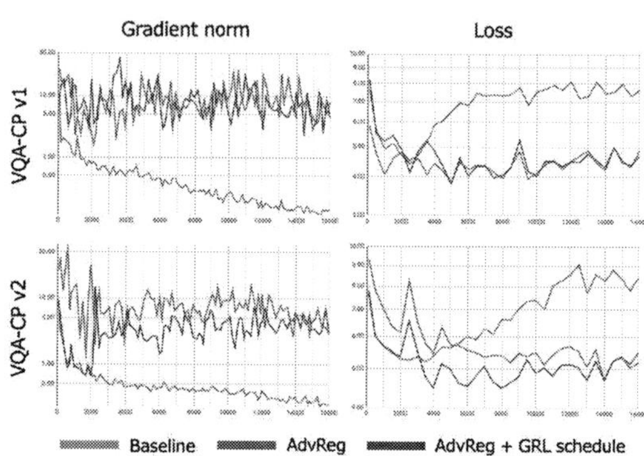

Figure 4: Gradient norms and loss during adversarial training. On VQA-CP v2, GRL scheduling helps to reduce gradient noise early in training (bottom left), leading to lower loss values (bottom right). On VQA-CP v1, the baseline (blue, top right) overfits more quickly; hence, delaying the regularization is less effective.

pecially those with fewer warm-up iterations, diverged due to exploding gradients. These findings suggest that the stronger the biases in a dataset, the earlier AdvReg must be introduced in order to counter overfitting effectively.

6 Error Analysis

We performed quantitative and qualitative error analyses to understand how AdvReg affects model inferences on different kinds of examples. To best highlight the effect of AdvReg, both analyses were performed on VQA-CP v1 test, where the change in priors is more pronounced. In both analyses, we compare our best AdvReg model (which did not use GRL scheduling) and the baseline model.

6.1 Quantitative Analysis

We first explore how model performance differs by question type. In the VQA datasets, each ques-

	AdvReg $\gg$ Baseline						AdvReg $\ll$ Baseline				
Question type	Ans.	N	Base.	Reg.	Δ	Question type	Ans.	N	Base.	Reg.	Δ
is there a	Yes/No	6501	16.75	93.41	49.83	is this	Yes/No	13063	76.96	64.85	-15.82
is this a	Yes/No	7177	29.70	86.27	40.60	what color is the	Other	4418	47.71	21.36	-11.64
are the	Yes/No	5037	24.99	87.07	31.27	what	Other	8646	38.48	25.28	-11.42
does the	Yes/No	3525	24.02	94.34	24.79	what is the	Other	6363	41.49	28.51	-8.26
is	Yes/No	3154	32.84	92.38	18.78	is the	Other	1148	50.44	4.40	-5.29
are they	Yes/No	1577	27.96	89.40	9.69	what kind of	Other	3141	51.43	35.51	-5.00
do you	Yes/No	1083	26.14	92.32	7.17	how many	Number	15917	15.90	13.01	-4.60
is there	Yes/No	5265	68.83	78.45	5.06	what type of	Other	1995	54.74	36.30	-3.68
is the person	Yes/No	757	41.64	92.46	3.85	none of the above	Other	2057	29.65	13.66	-3.29
how many people are	Number	2118	11.96	21.08	1.93	what color are the	Other	1435	56.93	35.74	-3.04

Table 2: Comparison of relative strengths and weaknesses of regularized and baseline models. The top 10 question types for which the regularized model outperforms the baseline are shown on the left, and vice versa on the right.

tion is assigned a type corresponding to the 64 most common prefixes (e.g., "Is there a...?") or "none of the above." Additionally, each example is given an answer type (Yes/No, Number, Other).[6]

To quantify the relative performance of the AdvReg and baseline models, we computed a difference metric, weighted by the number of questions N of the given type:

$$\Delta = \tfrac{N}{100}\left(\text{score}_{\text{baseline}} - \text{score}_{\text{regularized}}\right)$$

Table 2 shows the question types with the largest and smallest Δ values, respectively. Compared to the baseline, the AdvReg model excels at Yes/No examples, but suffers on Other examples. Overall, AdvReg improves Yes/No test performance by 35.06 points, but reduces Other performance by 15.74 points (Table 1). Additionally, AdvReg reduces Number test performance by 0.95%, though in general both models score poorly on counting questions—a known shortcoming of many VQA models (Chattopadhyay et al., 2017; Trott et al., 2018; Zhang et al., 2018).

These results suggest that much of the observed advantage of AdvReg on VQA-CP test is due to the extreme biases present in the dataset. In VQA-CP, Yes/No questions encode very strong priors (e.g., "no" is the answer to roughly 90% of the questions beginning with "Is there a...?" in the v1 training set). Because this prior is inverted, any learned association between question prefixes and answers becomes harmful at test time. That AdvReg scores well above chance (77.64%) on Yes/No examples suggests that this model has, to a certain degree, learned to answer binary questions without relying on language priors.

In contrast, the 15.74% drop on Other-type examples implies that AdvReg impairs the model's ability to make inferences about questions with heterogeneous answers. Other-type questions typically have 3–20 top answers. This finding suggests that AdvReg interferes with learning of language cues in the question that yield key information about the answer.

6.2 Qualitative Analysis

In this section, we examine individual examples to highlight common success and failure modes of AdvReg. We consider different question types and compare the prior answer distribution in the train/test sets to the posterior distribution assigned by the AdvReg and baseline models. Expanding on the visualization format introduced by Ramakrishnan et al. (2018, Fig. 3), Fig. 5 shows examples where the AdvReg model successfully answered the question while the baseline model was wrong. In these cases, the baseline model prediction relies on the prior answer distribution in the train set, while the AdvReg model is able to overcome these priors to infer the correct answer.

Turning to failures, we investigate what kinds of errors the AdvReg model makes on Other-type examples—the largest source of errors according to Section 6.1. We randomly selected instances where the regularized model produced an incorrect answer, and manually grouped these examples into four approximate categories corresponding to different failure modes. Fig. 6 shows representative examples for each of these failure modes; more examples are available in Appendix A.3.

Fig. 6a shows an example where the regularized model fails to infer the correct form of the answer from the question, answering "beach" to a question that entails animal answers. In Fig. 6b, the regularized model struggles with a question that

---

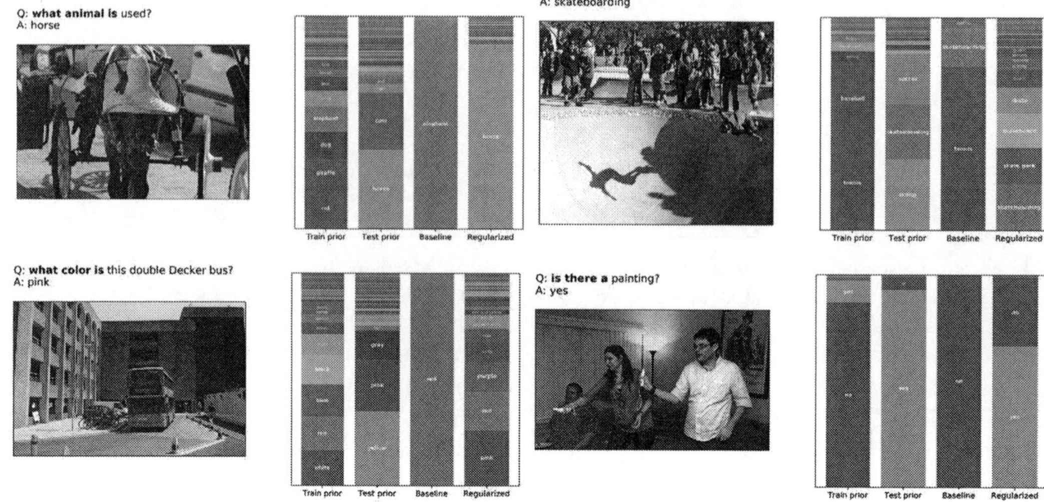

Figure 5: Visualization of AdvReg success cases. In each example, the leftmost two bars show the prior distribution over answers for the given question type (in bold). The rightmost two bars show the scores assigned to different answers by the baseline and AdvReg models for a particular example of the given type. The baseline model frequently assigns high probability to incorrect answers that are prominent in the training distribution. In contrast, the regularized model is able to make correct inferences in cases where the ground truth answer has low prior probability. Additional examples are provided in Appendix A.3.

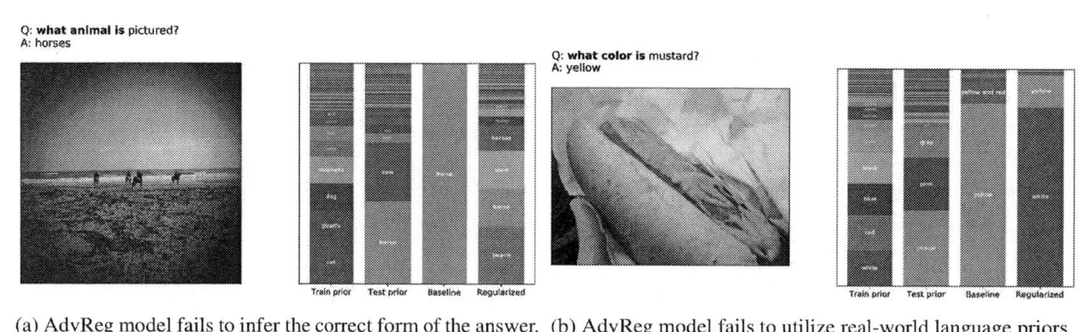

(a) AdvReg model fails to infer the correct form of the answer. (b) AdvReg model fails to utilize real-world language priors.

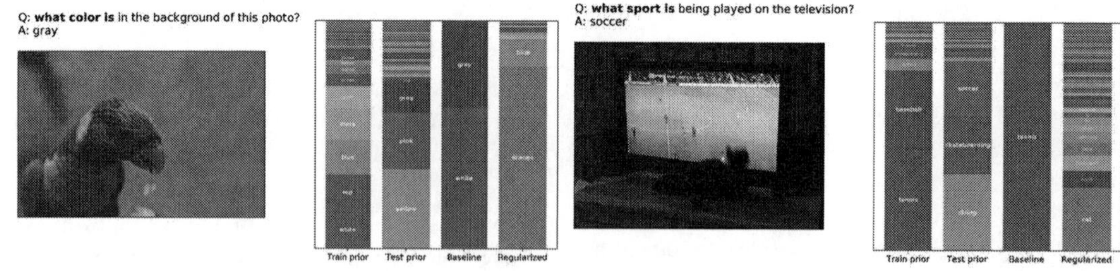

(c) AdvReg model distracted by visually-salient image features. (d) AdvReg model relies on image features, while baseline model relies on language priors.

Figure 6: Common failure modes of adversarial regularization. Additional examples are provided in Appendix A.3.

relies on real-world language priors (i.e., mustard is yellow). In Fig. 6c, the parrot's salient orange color distracts the regularized model from attending to the correct image region. Fig. 6d shows an example where the regularized model relies on visual features (the cat), while the baseline relies on language priors (tennis is a common answer to sport questions). These findings suggest that AdvReg may encourage models to rely on visual features at the expense of learning to interpret task-relevant linguistic information.

7 Conclusion

In this work, we investigated several strengths and limitations of adversarial regularization, a recently introduced technique for reducing language biases in VQA models. Though we find AdvReg improves performance on out-of-domain examples in VQA-CP, one concern is that the pendulum has swung too far: there are both quantitative and qualitative signs that our models are over-regularized. Quantitatively, the performance of our AdvReg models suffers on in-domain examples in VQA-CP and the original VQA datasets. Additionally, while AdvReg boosts performance on binary questions, it impairs performance on other question types. Qualitatively, we observe that AdvReg models draw on salient image features while ignoring important linguistic cues in questions. These results demonstrate that AdvReg interferes with certain key aspects of reasoning.

Our findings highlight the need for further research in two areas: datasets and modeling. The lack of a validation set in VQA-CP makes it difficult to perform hyperparameter tuning in a principled way. Moreover, the exaggerated biases in the existing VQA-CP splits may encourage over-regularization, as evidenced by the sharp discrepancy between AdvReg performance on binary and non-binary question types. To address these issues, future iterations of VQA-CP could contain three or more splits with moderate but distinct ratios of Yes/No answers. Restructuring VQA-CP in this way would help balance the importance of binary and non-binary questions, while providing researchers with more sound evaluation metrics.

On the modeling side, our findings suggest that AdvReg requires further refinement to avoid impairing learning of task-relevant linguistic information. One possible approach would be to use attention to apply different amounts of regulariza-tion to different words in the question. In this way, regularization could be focused on the first few words of the question (e.g., "Is there a...?") that encode answer distribution biases, while preserving other useful linguistic information. Such enhancements could lead to more targeted regularization techniques that preserve the benefits of AdvReg while reducing the drawbacks discussed in this work.

Acknowledgements

We would like to thank Alexander Rush for providing helpful advice and comments throughout our work on this project. GG and YB were supported by the Harvard Mind, Brain, and Behavior Initiative.

References

Aishwarya Agrawal, Dhruv Batra, and Devi Parikh. 2016. Analyzing the Behavior of Visual Question Answering Models. In *EMNLP*, pages 1955–1960.

Aishwarya Agrawal, Dhruv Batra, Devi Parikh, and Aniruddha Kembhavi. 2018. Don't Just Assume; Look and Answer: Overcoming Priors for Visual Question Answering. In *CVPR*, pages 4971–4980.

Peter Anderson, Xiaodong He, Chris Buehler, Damien Teney, Mark Johnson, Stephen Gould, and Lei Zhang. 2018. Bottom-Up and Top-Down Attention for Image Captioning and Visual Question Answering. In *CVPR*, volume 3, page 6.

Stanislaw Antol, Aishwarya Agrawal, Jiasen Lu, Margaret Mitchell, Dhruv Batra, C Lawrence Zitnick, and Devi Parikh. 2015. VQA: Visual Question Answering. In *ICCV*, pages 2425–2433.

Yonatan Belinkov, Adam Poliak, Stuart M. Shieber, Benjamin Van Durme, and Alexander Rush. 2019. On Adversarial Removal of Hypothesis-only Bias in Natural Language Inference. In *The Eighth Joint Conference on Lexical and Computational Semantics (*SEM)*.

Wei-Lun Chao, Hexiang Hu, and Fei Sha. 2018. Being Negative but Constructively: Lessons Learnt from Creating Better Visual Question Answering Datasets. In *NAACL-HLT*, volume 1, pages 431–441.

Prithvijit Chattopadhyay, Ramakrishna Vedantam, Ramprasaath R Selvaraju, Dhruv Batra, and Devi Parikh. 2017. Counting Everyday Objects in Everyday Scenes. In *CVPR*, pages 1135–1144.

Carsten Eickhoff. 2018. Cognitive Biases in Crowdsourcing. In *WSDM*, pages 162–170. ACM.

Yaroslav Ganin, Evgeniya Ustinova, Hana Ajakan, Pascal Germain, Hugo Larochelle, François Laviolette, Mario Marchand, and Victor Lempitsky. 2016. Domain-Adversarial Training of Neural Networks. *JMLR*, 17(1):2096–2030.

Yash Goyal, Tejas Khot, Douglas Summers-Stay, Dhruv Batra, and Devi Parikh. 2017. Making the V in VQA matter: Elevating the Role of Image Understanding in Visual Question Answering. In *CVPR*, pages 6904–6913.

Suchin Gururangan, Swabha Swayamdipta, Omer Levy, Roy Schwartz, Samuel Bowman, and Noah A. Smith. 2018. Annotation Artifacts in Natural Language Inference Data. In *NAACL-HLT*, pages 107–112, New Orleans, Louisiana. Association for Computational Linguistics.

Lisa Anne Hendricks, Kaylee Burns, Kate Saenko, Trevor Darrell, and Anna Rohrbach. 2018. Women also Snowboard: Overcoming Bias in Captioning Models. In *ECCV*, pages 771–787.

Allan Jabri, Armand Joulin, and Laurens van der Maaten. 2016. Revisiting Visual Question Answering Baselines. In *ECCV*, pages 727–739. Springer.

Yu Jiang, Vivek Natarajan, Xinlei Chen, Marcus Rohrbach, Dhruv Batra, and Devi Parikh. 2018a. Pythia. https://github.com/facebookresearch/pythia.

Yu Jiang, Vivek Natarajan, Xinlei Chen, Marcus Rohrbach, Dhruv Batra, and Devi Parikh. 2018b. Pythia v0.1: The Winning Entry to the VQA Challenge 2018. *arXiv preprint arXiv:1807.09956*.

Justin Johnson, Bharath Hariharan, Laurens van der Maaten, Li Fei-Fei, C Lawrence Zitnick, and Ross Girshick. 2017. CLEVR: A Diagnostic Dataset for Compositional Language and Elementary Visual Reasoning. In *CVPR*, pages 1988–1997. IEEE.

Divyansh Kaushik and Zachary C. Lipton. 2018. How Much Reading Does Reading Comprehension Require? A Critical Investigation of Popular Benchmarks. In *EMNLP*, pages 5010–5015, Brussels, Belgium. ACL.

Tsung-Yi Lin, Michael Maire, Serge Belongie, James Hays, Pietro Perona, Deva Ramanan, Piotr Dollár, and C Lawrence Zitnick. 2014. Microsoft COCO: Common Objects in Context. In *ECCV*, pages 740–755. Springer.

Emiel van Miltenburg. 2016. Stereotyping and Bias in the Flickr30k Dataset. *arXiv preprint arXiv:1605.06083*.

Ishan Misra, C Lawrence Zitnick, Margaret Mitchell, and Ross Girshick. 2016. Seeing Through the Human Reporting Bias: Visual Classifiers from Noisy Human-Centric Labels. In *CVPR*, pages 2930–2939.

Adam Poliak, Jason Naradowsky, Aparajita Haldar, Rachel Rudinger, and Benjamin Van Durme. 2018. Hypothesis Only Baselines in Natural Language Inference. In **SEM*, pages 180–191, New Orleans, Louisiana. ACL.

Sainandan Ramakrishnan, Aishwarya Agrawal, and Stefan Lee. 2018. Overcoming Language Priors in Visual Question Answering with Adversarial Regularization. In *NIPS*, pages 1548–1558.

Roy Schwartz, Maarten Sap, Ioannis Konstas, Leila Zilles, Yejin Choi, and Noah A. Smith. 2017. Story Cloze Task: UW NLP System. In *LSDSem*.

Damien Teney, Peter Anderson, Xiaodong He, and Anton van den Hengel. 2018. Tips and Tricks for Visual Question Answering: Learnings from the 2017 Challenge. In *CVPR*, pages 4223–4232.

Jesse Thomason, Daniel Gordan, and Yonatan Bisk. 2018. Shifting the Baseline: Single Modality Performance on Visual Navigation & QA. *arXiv preprint arXiv:1811.00613*.

Alexander Trott, Caiming Xiong, and Richard Socher. 2018. Interpretable Counting for Visual Question Answering. In *ICLR*.

Masatoshi Tsuchiya. 2018. Performance Impact Caused by Hidden Bias of Training Data for Recognizing Textual Entailment. In *LREC*.

Peng Zhang, Yash Goyal, Douglas Summers-Stay, Dhruv Batra, and Devi Parikh. 2016. Yin and Yang: Balancing and Answering Binary Visual Questions. In *CVPR*, pages 5014–5022. IEEE.

Yan Zhang, Jonathon Hare, and Adam Prgel-Bennett. 2018. Learning to Count Objects in Natural Images for Visual Question Answering. In *ICLR*.

Jieyu Zhao, Tianlu Wang, Mark Yatskar, Vicente Ordonez, and Kai-Wei Chang. 2017. Men Also Like Shopping: Reducing Gender Bias Amplification using Corpus-level Constraints. In *EMNLP*.

A Appendix

A.1 Implementation Details

Here, we provide additional details of our implementation. We experimented with different numbers of hidden layers $N = 1, 2, 3$ and hidden units $h = 256, 512, 1024, 2048$ in the adversarial classifier. We found the details of the adversary architecture to have little impact on performance, with the exception that adversaries with $N > 1$ hidden layers were more effective than one-layer adversaries. Both the adversary and the base VQA model are randomly initialized with a fixed seed at the start of training. We co-train the networks for 16k iterations with two separate PyTorch Adamax optimizers with batch size 512 and learning rate 0.001. Unlike Jiang et al. (2018b), we keep the learning rate fixed throughout training to minimize the possibility of gradient scaling mismatch between the base model and the adversary. While this modification causes the performance of the baseline VQA model to drop 1.1%, it greatly improves stability and convergence during adversarial training.

A.2 GRL Scheduling Details

For both VQA-CP v1 and v2, we performed a grid search to determine the optimal hyperparameters μ and w for the GRL schedule. We tested all combinations of delay $\mu = 0, 1000, 2000, 3000, 4000, 5000, 6000$ and warmup duration $w = 1000, 2000, 3000, 4000$. Given that the baseline model demonstrates signs of overfitting on VQA-CP v1 as early as 2000 iterations into training, we tested an additional set of accelerated GRL schedules for VQA-CP v1 that consisted of all combinations of $\mu = 500, 1000, 1500, 2000, 2500, 3000, 3500$ and $w = 500, 1000, 2000, 4000$.

Sometimes when AdvReg is introduced on a delayed schedule (especially if the value of μ is large), overfitting occurs before AdvReg takes effect. To avoid ending training prematurely, we always train for at least μ iterations before early stopping can be triggered. For instance, if $\mu = 3000$, then the earliest that we will stop training is $t = 4000$. For the purposes of evaluation, we also consider only scores from $t > \mu$ when scoring models under GRL scheduling.

A.3 Additional Examples

Figure 7: Visualization of AdvReg success cases. In each example, the leftmost two bars show the prior distribution over answers for the given question type (in bold). The rightmost two bars show the scores assigned to different answers by the baseline and AdvReg models for a particular example of the given type. The baseline model frequently assigns high probability to incorrect answers that are prominent in the training distribution. In contrast, the regularized model is able to make correct inferences in cases where the ground truth answer has low prior probability.

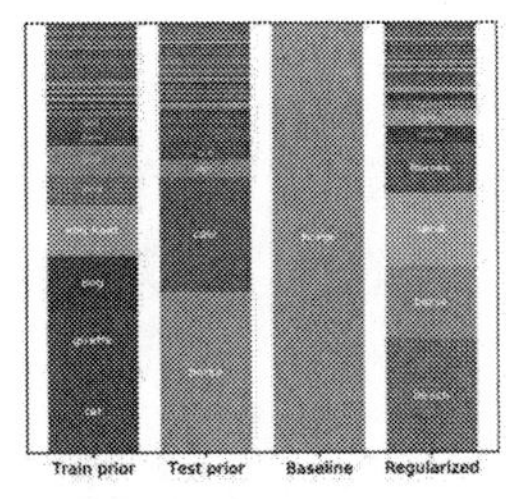

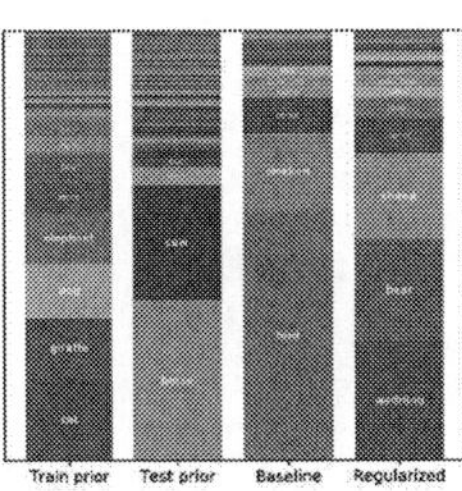

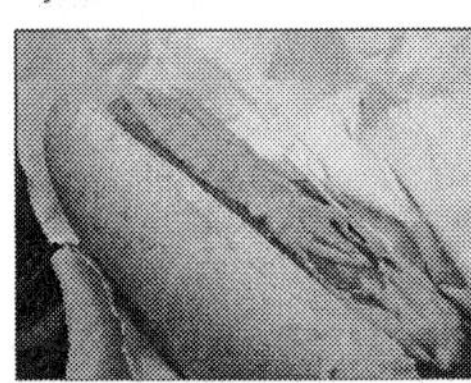

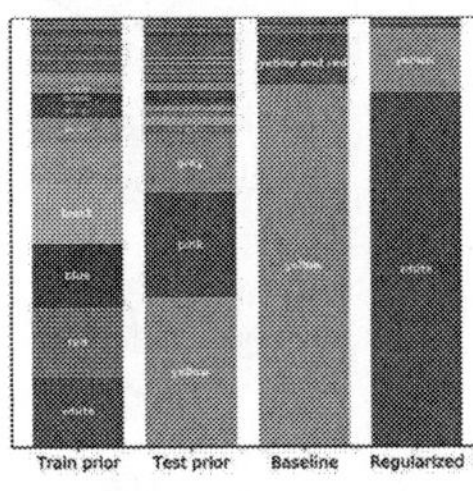

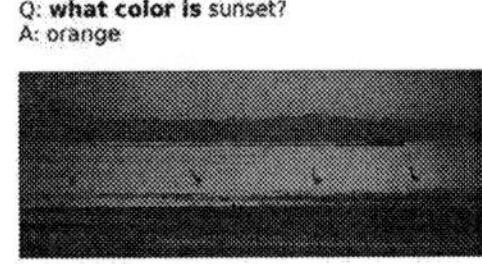

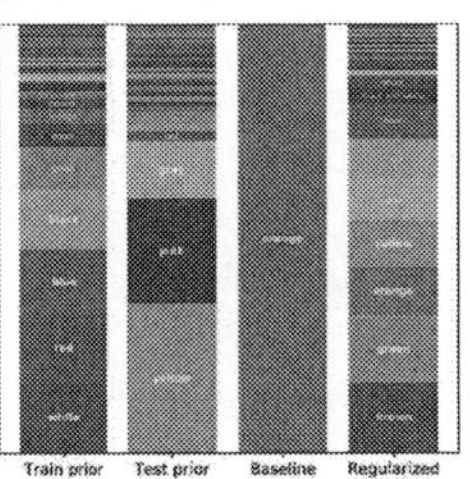

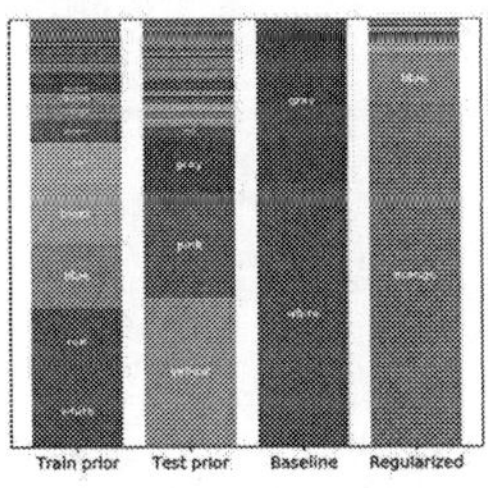

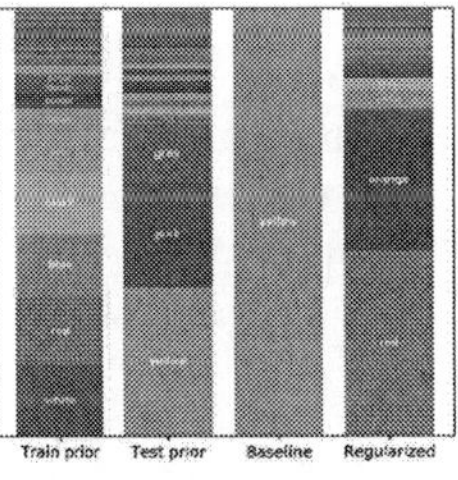

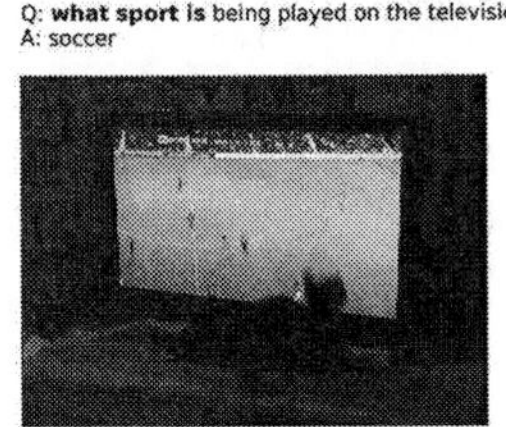

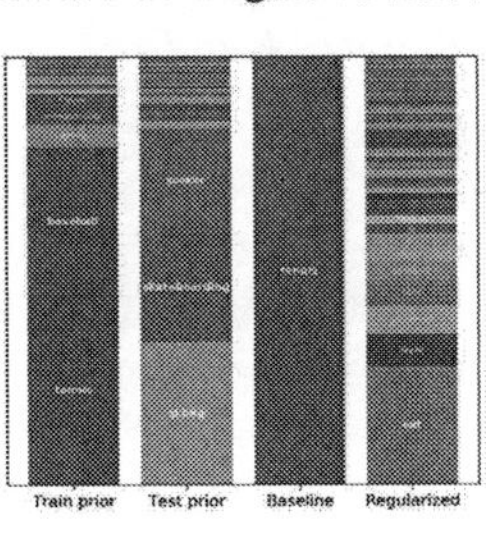

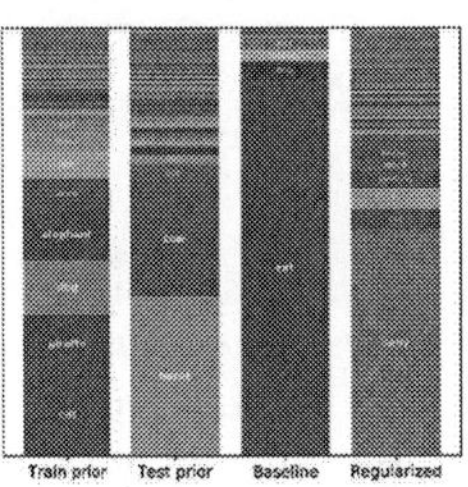

Figure 8: Common failure modes of adversarial regularization. First row: the regularized model fails to infer the correct form of the answer from the question, answering "beach" and "wedding" to questions that entail animal answers. Second row: the regularized model struggles with questions that rely on real-world language priors; i.e., mustard is yellow, sunset is orange. Third row: salient colors in the image distract the regularized model from attending to the correct image regions. Fourth row: both the baseline and regularized models perform poorly on questions where the answer relates to a localized image region (i.e., inside a TV) as opposed to the global image. In these cases, the regularized model relies on generic visual features in the image in its inferences, while the baseline model relies on language priors.

Referring to Objects in Videos using
Spatio-Temporal Identifying Descriptions

Peratham Wiriyathammabhum♠◇, Abhinav Shrivastava♠◇,
Vlad I. Morariu◇, Larry S. Davis♠◇
University of Maryland: Department of Computer Science♠, UMIACS◇
peratham@cs.umd.edu, abhinav@cs.umd.edu
morariu@umd.edu, lsd@umiacs.umd.edu

Abstract

This paper presents a new task, the grounding of spatio-temporal identifying descriptions in videos. Previous work suggests potential bias in existing datasets and emphasizes the need for a new data creation schema to better model linguistic structure. We introduce a new data collection scheme based on grammatical constraints for surface realization to enable us to investigate the problem of grounding spatio-temporal identifying descriptions in videos. We then propose a two-stream modular attention network that learns and grounds spatio-temporal identifying descriptions based on appearance and motion. We show that motion modules help to ground motion-related words and also help to learn in appearance modules because modular neural networks resolve task interference between modules. Finally, we propose a future challenge and a need for a robust system arising from replacing ground truth visual annotations with automatic video object detector and temporal event localization.

1 Introduction

Localizing referring expressions in videos involves *both static and dynamic information*. A referring expression (Dale and Reiter, 1995; Roy and Reiter, 2005) is a linguistic expression that grounds its meaning to a specific referent object in the world. The input video can be very long, have unknown length, contain many objects from the same class, or contain similar actions and interactions throughout the video. A successful, grounded communication between a speaker and a listener must ensure that the sentence or discourse provides enough information such that the listener can eliminate all distractors and focus only on the referent object that acts in a specific time interval. That essential information varies from the diversity of events in the world. However, a speaker is

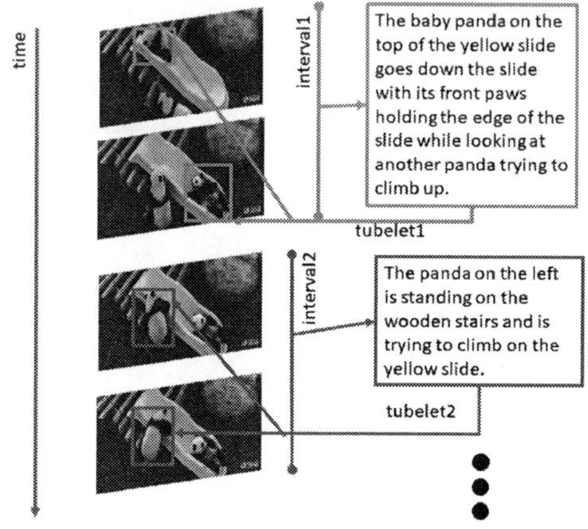

Figure 1: The first spatio-temporal identifying description in the green box grounds to the event that a panda goes down the slide. Another panda can be a context because they are interacting in the same scene. The second identifying description in the blue box grounds to the event that another panda climbs up the slide.

likely to mention salient properties and also salient differences based on the referent in comparison to other distractors. The differences can be about object category, attributes, poses, actions, changes in location, relationships and contexts in the scene.

Existing *image referring expression* datasets (Mao et al., 2016; Johnson et al., 2015; Kazemzadeh et al., 2014; Plummer et al., 2017; Krishna et al., 2017b) do not contain referring expressions that refer to dynamic properties or movements of the referent. These datasets do not require temporal understanding that would require a system to learn that "moving to the right" is different from "moving to the left" and "getting up" is different from "lying down". Existing *video referring expression* datasets and approaches (Krishna et al., 2017a; Hendricks et al., 2017; Gao et al., 2017; Berzak et al., 2015; Li et al., 2017; Hendricks et al., 2018; Gavrilyuk et al., 2018) focus only on temporal localization but referent

Proceedings of the Second Workshop on Shortcomings in Vision and Language, pages 14–25
Minneapolis, USA, June 6, 2019. ©2017 Association for Computational Linguistics

Two-stream Modular Attention Neural Network

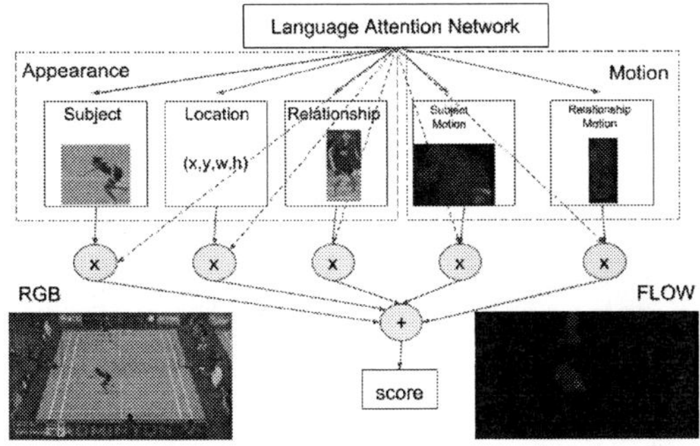

Figure 2: We add a motion stream to modular attention network. Our motion modules take optical flow input and model motion information for the subject and its relationship.

object localization. In other words, they do not ground events in both space and time. Emphasized by (Cirik et al., 2018), the data collection process for referring expressions should incorporate linguistic structure such that the model can learn more than shallow correlations between pairs of a sentence and visual features. That is, a particular dataset should not have a shortcut that only detecting nouns (object class) can perform well. Our dataset mitigates this issue by forcing instance-level recognition. We create a requirement that grounding the referring expressions must identify the target object among many distractors from the *contrast set* (same class distractors).

The contributions of this paper are (i) We propose a novel vision and language data collection scheme based on grammatical constraints for surface realization to ground video referring expressions in both space and time with lexical correlations between vision and language. We collected the ***Spatio-Temporal Video Identifying Description Localization (STV-IDL)*** dataset consisting of 199 video sequences from Youtube and 7,569 identifying descriptions. (ii) We propose an interpretable system based on ***two-stream modular attention network*** that models both appearance and motion to ground referring expressions as instance-level video object detection and event localization. We also perform ablation studies to get insights and identify potential challenges for the task.

2 Spatio-Temporal Localization

Given ground truth temporal intervals ($[start, end]$) and object tubelets (a sequence

of object bounding box coordinates in a given temporal interval, $\{[x_0, y_0, x_1, y_1]_{start}, \ldots,$ $[x_0, y_0, x_1, y_1]_{end}\}$), we want to localize an identifying expression ie to the correct target tubelet tb_{target} not the distractor tubelets $tb_{distractor}$ as our predicted tubelet r. We evaluate using the accuracy measure.

For automatic localization, tubelet IoU (Russakovsky et al., 2015) and temporal IoU are used to evaluate the bounding box and temporal interval with the ground truth respectively. Let R_i be the region in the frame i to be detected,

$$tubelet\ IoU = \frac{\sum_i \delta(IoU(r_i, R_i) > 0.5)}{N}, \quad (1)$$

where the denominator is the number of detected frame measured by the standard Intersection over Union (IoU) in an image and N denotes the number of union frames.

$$temporal\ IoU = \frac{\cap(interval_i, interval_j)}{\cup(interval_i, interval_j)}, \quad (2)$$

where $interval_i$ and $interval_j$ are input temporal intervals and the intersection and union functions are operations over 1-D intervals.

3 Related Work

Spatio-Temporal Localization. Spatio-temporal localization (or action understanding) is a long standing challenge in computer vision. Most existing datasets like LIRIS-HARL (Wolf et al., 2014), J-HMDB (Jhuang et al., 2013), UCF-Sports (Rodriguez et al., 2008), UCF-101 (Soomro et al., 2012) or AVA (Gu et al., 2018) localize a spatio-temporal tubelet for human actions in either trimmed videos or a simple visual setting or a fixed lexicon. In contrast to action labels, our work accepts a free-form referring expression annotation which also contains a richer set of relations in the forms of prepositions, adverbs and conjunctions.

Referring Expression Comprehension. The goal of referring expression comprehension (Golland et al., 2010) is to ground phrases or sentences into the specific visual regions that the phrase refers. Prior works in the image domain have either focused on using a captioning module to generate the sentence (Mao et al., 2016; Nagaraja et al., 2016) or learning a joint embedding to comprehend the sentence by modeling the corresponding region unambiguously and localize the region

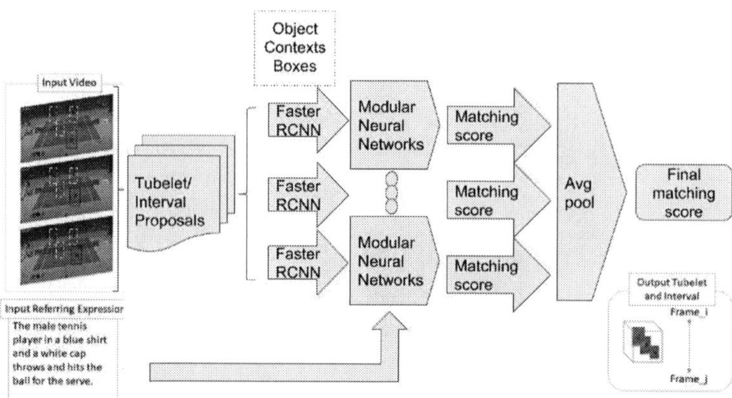

Figure 3: An overview of our system: an input video is using either ground truth annotations or is fed into both tubelet object proposal and temporal interval proposal modules. The resulting tubelet and interval proposals are then fed into an appearance and motion Faster-RCNN to extract the two-stream features. Then, a modular neural network will rank the tubelets given an input referring expression. The scores are average-pooled, and the system outputs the most likely tubelet that contains the reference object.

(Rohrbach et al., 2016; Wang et al., 2016; Hu et al., 2017; Yu et al., 2018). For the video domain, (Yamaguchi et al., 2017) further annotated the ActivityNet dataset with one referring expression per video for video retrieval with natural language query. (Li et al., 2017) uses referring expressions to help track a target object in a video sequence in a subset of OTB100 (Lu et al., 2014) and ImageNet VID (Russakovsky et al., 2015). DiDeMo (Hendricks et al., 2017) and TEMPO (Hendricks et al., 2018) focus on localizing an input sentence into the corresponding temporal interval out of a finite number of backgrounds. Importantly, these datasets do not consider distractor objects from the same class. While our work also focuses on the video domain, it focuses on localizing objects and events as spatio-temporal tubelets aligned with an input expression.

Surface Realization in Vision and Language. Surface realization is a process for generating surface forms, like natural language sentences, based on some underlying representations. For natural language generation, the underlying representation tends to be syntactic features. In vision and language, captioning systems can use meaning representation like triplets as an input for a surface realization module to generate a sentence. (Farhadi et al., 2010) uses <Objects, Actions, Scenes>. (Yang et al., 2011) uses part-of-speech as <Nouns, Verbs, Scenes, Prepositions>. (Li et al., 2011) uses <<adj1, obj1>, prep, <adj2, obj2>>where adjectives are object attributes and prepositions are spatial relationships between ob-

jects. TEMPO (Hendricks et al., 2018) and TVQA (Lei et al., 2018) use a compositional format for words like before or after to specify temporal relationships between events during crowdsourcing.

We incorporate grammatical constraints (Linguistic prescription) based on part-of-speech into our annotation pipeline so that we can crowdsource well-formed sentences from people which contain enough meaning representations for vision systems to locate the target object with visual contexts. Instead of manually writing sentences based on context-free grammars like (Yu and Siskind, 2013), we ask the annotators to write sentences in which valid sentences contain at least a noun phrase (NP), a verb phrase (VP) and one of a prepositional phrase (PP), adverb phrase (ADVP) or conjunction phrase (CONJP). The rest of each sentence are language variations where we expect crowdsourcing to create more variations compared to manual annotations by a few annotators. We want computer vision models to learn useful and interpretable features by correlating the expressions and videos. So, we want the learned visual semantics from grounding models to be similar to structural inputs in surface realization systems. Each part-of-speech correlates with a specific visual feature.

4 STV-IDL Dataset

4.1 Dataset Construction

We develop a new data collection schema that ensures rich correspondences between referring ex-

Table 1: STV-IDL dataset statistics.

Info	Statistics
Number of Videos	199
Number of Sentences	7569
Average objects per Video	2.85
Average words per Sentence	22.65
Sentences per Video	38.04

Table 2: STV-IDL part-of-speech statistics. (Please see the supplementary material for more details.)

Part-of-Speech	percents
Noun, singular or mass (NN)	28.1
Determiner (DT)	15.3
Preposition or subordinating conjunction (IN)	10.9
Adjective (JJ)	9.7
Possessive pronoun ($PRP)	5.7
Verb, 3rd person singular present (VBZ)	5.1
Adverbs (RB)	3.6
Coordinating conjunction (CC)	3.4

pressions and referred objects in a video using constraints. The spatio-temporal relations that we are interested in are about state transitions, that is, what happens before and after the action and how objects move. The state transitions should be relative to other objects and background. For example, a sentence *'A man in a green uniform kicking the ball then running toward the net.'* is a good video referring expression. This sentence is valid only in a spatial region that represents a noun phrase *'a man in a green uniform'* and a time interval in which an action from the verb phrase *'hitting the ball then running toward the net'* occurs. Also, the action *'hitting the ball'* comes before his next action *'running toward the net'* which shows the action steps of *'hitting'* followed by *'running'* and the action *'running'* has a context object *'the net.'*

First, we ensure that all of our High Definition videos (720p) crawled from Youtube contain at least two objects similar to (Mao et al., 2016), but each video will focus on just one object class to form a contrast set. This constraint prevents a simple video object detector from resolving referential ambiguity using only nouns by just outputting based on class information as in (Cirik et al., 2018). Because a simple object detector randomly outputs one object from a combination of the target and the contrast set. Then, the output is the same as random because the object confidence scores do not correlate with the referring expression. We want more language cues to guide the system to seek additional visual contexts (Divvala et al., 2009) to focus and output *only one* unambiguous object detection. The dataset contains 13 categories of videos which are either multi-player sports or animals. Second, inspired by (Siskind, 1990; Yu and Siskind, 2013), a sentence, consists of a subject and a predicate, can be viewed as a set of structured labels based on part-of-speech and each label can be meaningfully grounded in a video. Besides, annotations can use *grammars for lexical grounding and surface real-*

ization. Therefore, we ensure that every referring expression in our dataset provides grammatically relevant visual grounding based on part-of-speech such that a valid sentence must contain at least a noun phrase (NP), a verb phrase (VP) and one of a prepositional phrase (PP), adverb phrase (ADVP) or conjunction phrase (CONJP). We also found that the annotators may write relevant sentences without the constraints but the contents are random and may not be visually grounded either spatially or temporally or both in the video. Some example sentences without the constraints are *"The guy was lucky to save the tennis ball."* and *"The sun is blocking the ball for the back player."*.

4.2 Video Tubelet, Temporal Interval, and Expressions Annotations

We manually identify interesting events in each video and select a keyframe for that action in the presence of distractors. Then, we manually annotate the start and end of that event into an interval lasting around one second. For bounding box annotation, we use a javascript variant of Vatic (Vondrick et al., 2013; Bolkensteyn) to manually draw a tubelet of bounding boxes in all frames for each object of interest in every video. We crowdsource annotations of referring expressions from Amazon Mechanical Turk (AMT). We create a clip segment with a bounding box around the target object to fixate the annotator's attention.

Next, we manually verify the referring expressions using another web interface that helps us evaluate if the sentence refers to the target object, is correct based on the video, is different from sentences for the distractors and is sufficient to distinguish the target object from the distractors and the

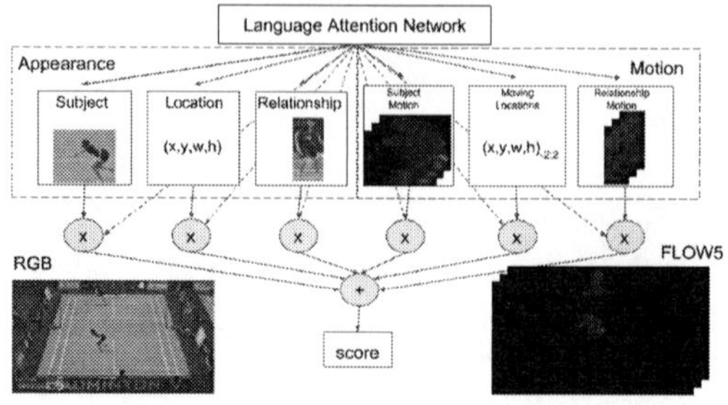

Figure 4: Stacked two-stream modular attention network based on five optical flow image input. We model the bounding box sequence is a moving location module and a relationship module. The motion Faster-RCNN is also trained using a stack of five flow images for frame index $f_i \in [t-2, t+2]$.

background. The annotation interfaces, payment and dataset statistics are shown in supplementary material. We refer to the resulting referring expressions as *identifying descriptions* (Mitchell et al., 2013) because our expressions are referring expressions in the verified intervals which may be overspecified but are also descriptions which may be underspecified for the whole videos. Our referring expressions are long because we want to make sure that they are clear enough to provide input cues for the system. However, it still might be not enough to localize an event from the whole video because the video has many events and can be exhaustive to be specific for a particular event.

5 Approach: Two-stream Modular Attention Network

We start by employing a state-of-the-art image referring expression localization, namely, Modular Attention Network (MAttNet) (Yu et al., 2018) for our tasks. This model fits our objective since it is a variant of modular neural networks (Auda and Kamel, 1999; Andreas et al., 2016) that is decomposed based on tasks according to Fodor's modularity of mind (Fodor, 1985). Therefore, we can interpret the model in an ablation study on each neural module for a specific vision subtask and input type. Also, the model also provides linguistic interpretability using its language attention module that can visualize different bindings from word symbols in a referring expression to each visual module as attention $a_{m,t}$ where module $m \in \{subj, loc, rel\}$ (subject, location, rela-

tionship) and t is the index location of the word this attention weights its hidden representation the Bi-LSTM encodes.

The original MAttNet model (RGB) decomposes image referring expression grounding into three modules, a subject module, a location module, and a relationship module. The network output score for an object o_i and an expression r is,

$$S(o_i|r) = \sum_{m \in modules} w_m S(o_i|q^m), \qquad (3)$$

where w_m is the weight vector from the language attention module on the visual module m. q^m is the weighted sum of attention $a_{m,t}$ over all word embedding. $S(o_i|q^m)$ is the module score from a cosine similarity in the joint embedding between the visual representation of o_i denoted as $\widetilde{v}_i^m$ and q^m.

Given a positive pair (o_i, r_i), the network is discriminatively trained by sampling two negative pairs (o_i, r_j) and (o_k, r_i) where r_j is the expression from other contrast object and o_k is the contrast object from the same frame. The combined hinged loss L_r is,

$$L_r = \sum_i \lambda_1 \max(0, \Delta + S(o_i, r_j) - S(o_i, r_i))$$

$$+ \lambda_2 \max(0, \Delta + S(o_k, r_i) - S(o_i, r_i)). \quad (4)$$

The loss is linearly combined with other loss terms such as attribute prediction with cross-entropy loss L_{att} from the subject module in a multi-task learning setting.

We extend MAttNet to the video domain by applying two things. First, MAttNet uses Faster-RCNN (Girshick, 2015) for feature extraction so we follow a well-established actor-action detection pipeline which extends image object detection to frame-based spatio-temporal action detection (Peng and Schmid, 2016). With this, we reframe the problem by replacing action labels with referring expressions and putting MAttNet on top of Faster-RCNN. Also, we use external object and interval proposal instead of Region Proposal Network (RPN) in Faster-RCNN. Second, we add subject motion and relationship motion modules to capture temporal information in a two-streams setting (Simonyan and Zisserman, 2014). These modules have the same architecture as the subject and relationship module but are using optical flow as their input. We replace the three channel RGB input with a stack of flow-x, flow-y and flow magnitude from the flow image. The aim of these modifications, depicted in Figure 2, is to better model attributes, motion, movements and dynamic context in a video.

Previous work (Simonyan and Zisserman, 2014) has shown that stacking many optical flow images can help recognition. So, we train another variant of two-stream modular attention network using stacked five optical flow frames shown in Figure 4. In this setting, we train the stacked motion Faster-RCNN by stacking flow images F_{idx} where frame index $idx \in [t-2, t+2]$. The input becomes a 15 channel stacked optical flow image. In addition, we add the moving location module to further model the movement of the location by stacking location features $l_i = [\frac{x_{min}}{W}, \frac{y_{min}}{H}, \frac{x_{max}}{W}, \frac{y_{max}}{H}, \frac{Area_{region}}{Area_{image}}]$ where W and H are width and height of the image. Then the location features are concatenated with the location difference feature of the target object with up to five context objects from the same class, $\delta_{ij} = [\frac{\Delta x_{min}}{W}, \frac{\Delta y_{min}}{H}, \frac{\Delta x_{max}}{W}, \frac{\Delta y_{max}}{H}, \frac{\Delta Area_{region}}{Area_{image}}]$ so that we have a sequence of $[l_i; \delta_{ij}]_{idx}$ where frame index $idx \in [t-2, t+2]$. Then, we place an LSTM on top of the sequence and we forward the concatenation of all hidden states to a fully connected layer and output the final location features. We also make a location sequence and place an LSTM on top of location in the relationship motion module in this stacked optical flow setting.

5.1 Tubelet and Temporal Interval Proposals

We employ the state-of-the-art video object detector, flow-guided feature aggregation (FGFA) (Zhu et al., 2017), finetuned on STV-IDL to generate the tubelet proposals. The per-frame detections from FGFA are post-processed by linking into tubelets using Seq-NMS (Han et al., 2016) based on the top 300 bounding boxes ranked by the confidence of the category scores.

For temporal proposals, we implemented a variant of Deep Action Proposals (DAPs) (Escorcia et al., 2016) based on multi-scale proposal. First, we use a temporal sliding window with a fixed length of L frames and a stride of s (8 in our case). This produces a set of intervals, (b_i, e_i) where b_i and e_i are the beginning and the end of the interval. Then, we extract the C3D features (Tran et al., 2015) from the image frames in that interval using the activation in the 'fc7' layer, pretrained

Table 3: Identifying Description Localization: mAP for each collection. (values are in percents.) The fused1 MAttNet is the proposed two-stream method and the fused5 MAttNet is the stacked version of the proposed two-stream method.

Model	mAP
random	29.68
RGB MAttNet	41.51
flow MAttNet	39.02
flow5 MAttNet	41.90
fused1 MAttNet	**44.66**
fused5 MAttNet	42.82

Table 4: Ablation study on fused1 MAttNet: mAP for each module combination. (values are in percents.)

Model	mAP
Subject+Location	44.46
+Relationship	44.46
+Subject Motion	44.46
+Relationship Motion	**44.66**

on the Sports-1M dataset (Karpathy et al., 2014). The feature set $f = C3D(t_i : t_i + \delta)$, $t_i \in [b_i, e_i]$ where $\delta = 16$ from the original pretrained model. The duration of each segment L_k also increases as a power of 2, that is $L_{k+1} = 2 * L_k$. The features are fed to a 2-layered LSTM to perform $\{Event/Background\}$ sequence classification.

6 Experiments and Analysis

We want to show how and to what extent modular attention networks ground input expressions with motion information in videos. So, we perform two sets of experiments, identifying description localization and automatic video object detector and temporal event localization. Similar to (Gu et al., 2018), we split the dataset into training, validation and test sets at the video level; that is, there are no overlapping video segments for every split. There are 159 training, 13 validation, and 27 test videos. The rough ratio is 12:1:2. Implementation details are in the supplementary material.

6.1 Identifying Description Localization

Setup. We perform three experiments, localization with ground truth annotations, module ablation study, and word attention study. First, we evaluate our model by selecting the target from a pool of candidate targets plus distractors. We compare five models based on input and modules. The five models are (1) MAttNet for RGB in-

Table 5: Ablation study on fused5 MAttNet: mAP for each module combination. (values are in percents.)

Model	mAP
Subject+Location	33.97
+Relationship	35.32
+Subject Motion	35.41
+Moving Location	**42.84**
+Relationship Motion	42.82

put (RGB MAttNet/original model/baseline); (2) MAttNet for flow image input (flow MAttNet); (3) MAttNet for stacked five flow image input (flow5 MAttNet); (4) two-stream MAttNet for RGB and flow image input (fused1 MAttNet) and (5) two-stream MAttNet for RGB and stacked five flow image input (fused5 MAttNet). Second, we interpret the model by setting the module score weights from language attention module to zeros for the modules we want to turn off in our ablation study. Third, we collect the statistics of the attention of each word from the input expressions in the test set to explain how and which kind of words each module attends.

Results. The accuracies in Table 3 show superior performance for stacked flow5 and two-streams models. The stacked flow5 model improves over the RGB baseline by 0.39% while two-stream fused1 and fused5 models have 3.15% and 1.31% improvement respectively. Both variants of two-stream models, fused1 and fused5, outperform all one-stream models, RGB, flow, and flow5. All models perform better than randomly selecting an object from the set of tubelets.

The accuracies in Table 4 show that each module in fused1 learns better since the modules in appearance stream alone have 2.95% improvements over the RGB only baseline. We further hypothesize that *the reason is the motion stream takes care of motion grounding so the appearance modules can learn better because of the separation of unrelated information into other modules. A modular neural network avoids internal interference between features by training each module independently and each module will masters its task more precisely (Auda and Kamel, 1999).* The additional relationship motion module also provides complementary information for the additional 0.20% improvement. The accuracies in Table 5 show that the stacked flow5 model focuses mostly on the moving location module which causes the overall improvement over the RGB baseline. *The mov-*

ing location is a predictive feature to model motion and spatial location (Yin and Ordonez, 2017), but it prevents other vision modules from becoming sufficiently tuned in this setting. We also try to combine the moving location with the fused1 setting. The results degenerate more, and the overall accuracy is only 37.12%. It is even lower than flow MAttNet model.

Figure 6 shows how the language attention network assigns weights to each module by aggregating all the weights for each word based on Penn part-of-speech tag during test set prediction of the fused1 model to explain the performance gain. The aggregated statistics show that motion words like verbs, prepositions, and conjunctions are ranked higher for flow modules on average which means more attention to motion. We also focus on just aggregating verbs in Figure 7 to further explain the modules. The statistics show that flow and location modules focus more on verbs on average compared to their corresponding appearance-based modules.

6.2 Automatic Video Object Detector and Temporal Event Localization

Because spatio-temporal detection and localization is very challenging, we want to identify potential challenges for spatio-temporal grounding when automatic computer vision systems replace the ground truth annotations. So, we replace tubelets with top 8 detections from flow-guided feature aggregation (FGFA) (Zhu et al., 2017) and temporal intervals with the proposal system described in Section 3.2. We create three scenarios: in each scenario, varying amounts of the problem are revealed via the ground truth to separate each component and measure the hardness of each subproblem and the impact of one on another.

6.2.1 Automatic Video Object Detector

Setup. We evaluate both the tubelet object proposals and the pretrained modular attention networks. We replace the groundtruth tubelets to imperfect proposals which contains bounding box perturbations and we want to see how the model behaves.

Results. Since all modular attention networks are not trained on tubelet proposals, the results from the automatic video object detector in Table 6 shows performance drops in all models and the performances are even lower than the object detection baseline. The object detection baseline selects the tubelet with the highest confidence score

Figure 5: A qualitative result: the first, middle and last frames from an interval in the STV-IDL dataset with an expression, 'The male tennis player in the near court moves from right to left in order to hit the ball but his teammate outside the court reaches the ball first and just hits it.' The fused1 MAttNet can properly refer to the object highlighted in the red box in contrast to the baseline.

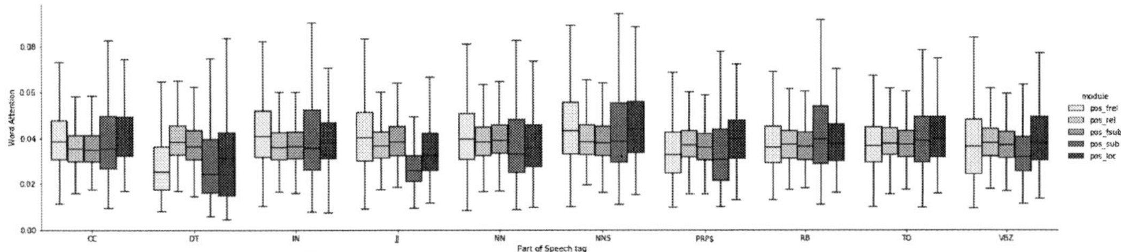

Figure 6: Aggregations of output word attention weights for each module on the STV-IDL test set. Part-of-speech tags are CC, DT, IN, JJ, NN, NNS, PRP\$, RB, TO and VBZ (left to right).

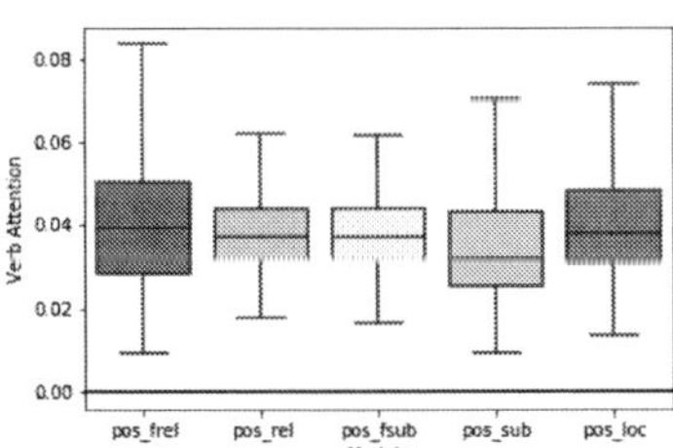

Figure 7: Aggregations on all verbs for each module. (from left to right: Relationship flow/RGB, Subject flow/RGB, Location)

Table 6: Visual Object Detection: mAP tracklet IoU@0.5 for each model. (values are in percents.)

Model	IoU@0.5
RGB MAttNet	**35.02**
flow MAttNet	22.63
flow5 MAttNet	28.98
fused1 MAttNet	23.93
fused5 MAttNet	24.26
FGFA most conf.	*35.87*
FGFA 2nd conf.	*34.16*

from FGFA. We hypothesize that it is from bounding box perturbation that may affect both Faster RCNN features and location features. The results also show that the performance drops are more severe in two-stream models - we think that it is from an accumulation of errors from both streams.

Table 7: Event Localization: mAP temporal IoU@0.5 for each model. (values are in percents.)

Model	tIoU@0.5
RGB MAttNet	8.72
flow MAttNet	7.28
flow5 MAttNet	**8.79**
fused1 MAttNet	8.07
fused5 MAttNet	7.02
speaker LSTM	7.74
speaker Bi-LSTM	**10.10**

6.2.2 Temporal Event Localization

Setup. We evaluate the event localization component by removing ground truth temporal intervals. All previous settings so far operate on trimmed video segments and focus on 'where' the sentences refer to. We want to see how the model behaves on untrimmed videos in which the system needs to answer 'when' the referred events occur. The system's task is to infer the temporal intervals $[t_k, t_{k+40})$ which are likely to correspond to the input expressions. We evaluate the system via temporal mean Average Precision with temporal IoU similar to (Krishna et al., 2017b). Since our identifying descriptions are sentences for the whole videos, we compare modular attention networks to a video captioner, S2VT (Venugopalan et al., 2015), which is a speaker model (Mao et al., 2016) that output the probability of producing an expression given a video. The S2VT model is trained

Table 8: Spatio-temporal Localization: mAP temporal IoU@0.5 then tracklet IoU@0.5 for each model. (values are in percents.)

Model	tIoU@0.5
RGB MAttNet	**2.75**
flow MAttNet	2.04
flow5 MAttNet	2.62
fused1 MAttNet	1.70
fused5 MAttNet	1.51

on a different feature set consisting of the image features from the last layer 'fc1000' of ResNet-50 (He et al., 2016), the interval (b_i, e_i) and the current frame number. This S2VT model is trained on ground truth intervals and expressions, so it is likely to produce expressions with high probabilities on the ground truth event intervals compared to the background intervals which do not contain 'interesting' events.

Results. The results in Table 7 shows that speaker Bi-LSTM performs the best and even better than all modular attention networks. We suspect that the reason is from the discriminative training scheme of the modular attention networks is not suitable for temporal localization. Training with only negative pairs from the same frame takes a week, so it is computationally expensive to train with all negative pairs from all frames in the whole video. The top-5 prediction for Bi-LSTM increases to 26.23% but it is still far from the upper bound of 71.02%, the recall of the proposal system.

6.2.3 Spatio-temporal Localization

Setup. We evaluate our event interval proposals, tubelet object proposals, and modular attention networks. We fix tubelet Intersection over Union (tubelet IoU) to 0.5. The evaluation is a two-step process, temporal IoU then tubelet IoU. We allow tubelet IoU over all frames of the proposal interval instead of ground truth interval to show that the system refers to the right object in an event interval and the tubelet IoU does not depend on temporal IoU.

Results. The results in Table 8 show that the performance further decreases from Table 7. We suspect that the reason is also from the discriminative training scheme because the models are not trained on some background frames.

7 Summary

We discussed the problem of grounding spatio-temporal identifying descriptions to spatio-temporal object-event tubelets in videos. The critical challenge in this dataset is to ground verbs and motion words in both space and time, and we show that this is possible by our proposed two-stream modular neural network models which have complimentary optical flow inputs to ground verbs and motion words. We validate this by collecting aggregated statistics on word attention and found that the two-stream models ground verbs better. The motion stream also helps the appearance stream learn better because it abstracts away motion noise from appearance. We further inspected the components in the system and revealed potential challenges. A better training scheme such as improved loss functions or hard example mining for future spatio-temporal grounding systems should consider both efficiency and effectiveness.

8 Acknowledgement

The authors thank the anonymous reviewers for their insightful comments and suggestions. We thank Dr. Hal Daumé III, Nelson Padua-Perez and Dr. Ryan Farrell for very useful advises and discussions. We also thank members of UMD Computer Vision Lab (CVL), UMD Human-Computer Interaction Lab (HCIL) and UMD Computational Linguistics and Information Processing Lab (CLIP) for useful insights and support. We also thank academic twitter users for useful knowledge and discussions.

References

Jacob Andreas, Marcus Rohrbach, Trevor Darrell, and Dan Klein. 2016. Neural module networks. In *Proceedings of the IEEE Conference on Computer Vision and Pattern Recognition*, pages 39–48.

Gasser Auda and Mohamed Kamel. 1999. Modular neural networks: a survey. *International Journal of Neural Systems*, 9(02):129–151.

Yevgeni Berzak, Andrei Barbu, Daniel Harari, Boris Katz, and Shimon Ullman. 2015. Do you see what i mean? visual resolution of linguistic ambiguities. In *Proceedings of the 2015 Conference on Empirical Methods in Natural Language Processing*, pages 1477–1487.

Dinesh Bolkensteyn. vatic.js: A pure javascript video annotation tool. https://dbolkensteyn.github.io/vatic.js/.

Volkan Cirik, Louis-Philippe Morency, and Taylor Berg-Kirkpatrick. 2018. Visual referring expression recognition: What do systems actually learn? In *Proceedings of the 2018 Conference of the North American Chapter of the Association for Computational Linguistics: Human Language Technologies, Volume 2 (Short Papers)*, volume 2, pages 781–787.

Robert Dale and Ehud Reiter. 1995. Computational interpretations of the gricean maxims in the generation of referring expressions. *Cognitive science*, 19(2):233–263.

Santosh K Divvala, Derek Hoiem, James H Hays, Alexei A Efros, and Martial Hebert. 2009. An empirical study of context in object detection. In *Computer Vision and Pattern Recognition, 2009. CVPR 2009. IEEE Conference on*, pages 1271–1278. IEEE.

Victor Escorcia, Fabian Caba Heilbron, Juan Carlos Niebles, and Bernard Ghanem. 2016. Daps: Deep action proposals for action understanding. In *European Conference on Computer Vision*, pages 768–784. Springer.

Ali Farhadi, Mohsen Hejrati, Mohammad Amin Sadeghi, Peter Young, Cyrus Rashtchian, Julia Hockenmaier, and David Forsyth. 2010. Every picture tells a story: Generating sentences from images. In *European conference on computer vision*, pages 15–29. Springer.

Jerry A Fodor. 1985. Precis of the modularity of mind. *Behavioral and brain sciences*, 8(1):1–5.

Jiyang Gao, Chen Sun, Zhenheng Yang, and Ram Nevatia. 2017. Tall: Temporal activity localization via language query. In *Proceedings of the IEEE International Conference on Computer Vision*, pages 5267–5275.

Kirill Gavrilyuk, Amir Ghodrati, Zhenyang Li, and Cees GM Snoek. 2018. Actor and action video segmentation from a sentence. In *Proceedings of the IEEE Conference on Computer Vision and Pattern Recognition*, pages 5958–5966.

Ross Girshick. 2015. Fast r-cnn. In *Proceedings of the IEEE international conference on computer vision*, pages 1440–1448.

Dave Golland, Percy Liang, and Dan Klein. 2010. A game-theoretic approach to generating spatial descriptions. In *Proceedings of the 2010 conference on empirical methods in natural language processing*, pages 410–419. Association for Computational Linguistics.

Chunhui Gu, Chen Sun, David Ross, Carl Vondrick, Caroline Pantofaru, Yeqing Li, Sudheendra Vijayanarasimhan, George Toderici, Susanna Ricco, Rahul Sukthankar, et al. 2018. Ava: A video dataset of spatio-temporally localized atomic visual actions. In *CVPR 2018*.

Wei Han, Pooya Khorrami, Tom Le Paine, Prajit Ramachandran, Mohammad Babaeizadeh, Honghui Shi, Jianan Li, Shuicheng Yan, and Thomas S Huang. 2016. Seq-nms for video object detection. *arXiv preprint arXiv:1602.08465*.

Kaiming He, Xiangyu Zhang, Shaoqing Ren, and Jian Sun. 2016. Deep residual learning for image recognition. In *Proceedings of the IEEE conference on computer vision and pattern recognition*, pages 770–778.

Lisa Anne Hendricks, Oliver Wang, Eli Shechtman, Josef Sivic, Trevor Darrell, and Bryan Russell. 2017. Localizing moments in video with natural language. In *Proceedings of the IEEE International Conference on Computer Vision (ICCV)*.

Lisa Anne Hendricks, Oliver Wang, Eli Shechtman, Josef Sivic, Trevor Darrell, and Bryan Russell. 2018. Localizing moments in video with temporal language. In *Proceedings of the 2018 Conference on Empirical Methods in Natural Language Processing*, pages 1380–1390.

Ronghang Hu, Marcus Rohrbach, Jacob Andreas, Trevor Darrell, and Kate Saenko. 2017. Modeling relationships in referential expressions with compositional modular networks. In *Computer Vision and Pattern Recognition (CVPR), 2017 IEEE Conference on*, pages 4418–4427. IEEE.

Hueihan Jhuang, Juergen Gall, Silvia Zuffi, Cordelia Schmid, and Michael J Black. 2013. Towards understanding action recognition. In *Proceedings of the IEEE international conference on computer vision*, pages 3192–3199.

Justin Johnson, Ranjay Krishna, Michael Stark, Li-Jia Li, David Shamma, Michael Bernstein, and Li Fei-Fei. 2015. Image retrieval using scene graphs. In *Proceedings of the IEEE Conference on Computer Vision and Pattern Recognition*, pages 3668–3678.

Andrej Karpathy, George Toderici, Sanketh Shetty, Thomas Leung, Rahul Sukthankar, and Li Fei-Fei. 2014. Large-scale video classification with convolutional neural networks. In *CVPR*.

Sahar Kazemzadeh, Vicente Ordonez, Mark Matten, and Tamara L Berg. 2014. Referitgame: Referring to objects in photographs of natural scenes. In *EMNLP*, pages 787–798.

Ranjay Krishna, Kenji Hata, Frederic Ren, Li Fei-Fei, and Juan Carlos Niebles. 2017a. Dense-captioning events in videos. In *International Conference on Computer Vision (ICCV)*.

Ranjay Krishna, Yuke Zhu, Oliver Groth, Justin Johnson, Kenji Hata, Joshua Kravitz, Stephanie Chen, Yannis Kalantidis, Li-Jia Li, David A Shamma, et al. 2017b. Visual genome: Connecting language and vision using crowdsourced dense image annotations. *International Journal of Computer Vision*, 123(1):32–73.

Jie Lei, Licheng Yu, Mohit Bansal, and Tamara Berg. 2018. Tvqa: Localized, compositional video question answering. In *Proceedings of the 2018 Conference on Empirical Methods in Natural Language Processing*, pages 1369–1379.

Siming Li, Girish Kulkarni, Tamara L Berg, Alexander C Berg, and Yejin Choi. 2011. Composing simple image descriptions using web-scale n-grams. In *Proceedings of the Fifteenth Conference on Computational Natural Language Learning*, pages 220–228. Association for Computational Linguistics.

Zhenyang Li, Ran Tao, Efstratios Gavves, Cees GM Snoek, Arnold WM Smeulders, et al. 2017. Tracking by natural language specification. In *CVPR*, volume 1, page 5.

Yang Lu, Tianfu Wu, and Song Chun Zhu. 2014. Online object tracking, learning and parsing with and-or graphs. In *Proceedings of the IEEE Conference on Computer Vision and Pattern Recognition*, pages 3462–3469.

Junhua Mao, Jonathan Huang, Alexander Toshev, Oana Camburu, Alan L Yuille, and Kevin Murphy. 2016. Generation and comprehension of unambiguous object descriptions. In *Proceedings of the IEEE conference on computer vision and pattern recognition*, pages 11–20.

Margaret Mitchell, Kees Van Deemter, and Ehud Reiter. 2013. Generating expressions that refer to visible objects. In *Proceedings of the 2013 Conference of the North American Chapter of the Association for Computational Linguistics*. Association for Computational Linguistics (ACL).

Varun K Nagaraja, Vlad I Morariu, and Larry S Davis. 2016. Modeling context between objects for referring expression understanding. In *European Conference on Computer Vision*, pages 792–807. Springer.

Xiaojiang Peng and Cordelia Schmid. 2016. Multi-region two-stream r-cnn for action detection. In *European Conference on Computer Vision*, pages 744–759. Springer.

Bryan A Plummer, Liwei Wang, Chris M Cervantes, Juan C Caicedo, Julia Hockenmaier, and Svetlana Lazebnik. 2017. Flickr30k entities: Collecting region-to-phrase correspondences for richer image-to-sentence models. *International Journal of Computer Vision*, 123(1):74–93.

Mikel D Rodriguez, Javed Ahmed, and Mubarak Shah. 2008. Action mach a spatio-temporal maximum average correlation height filter for action recognition. In *Computer Vision and Pattern Recognition, 2008. CVPR 2008. IEEE Conference on*, pages 1–8. IEEE.

Anna Rohrbach, Marcus Rohrbach, Ronghang Hu, Trevor Darrell, and Bernt Schiele. 2016. Grounding of textual phrases in images by reconstruction. In *European Conference on Computer Vision*, pages 817–834. Springer.

Deb Roy and Ehud Reiter. 2005. Connecting language to the world. *Artificial Intelligence*, 167(1-2):1–12.

Olga Russakovsky, Jia Deng, Hao Su, Jonathan Krause, Sanjeev Satheesh, Sean Ma, Zhiheng Huang, Andrej Karpathy, Aditya Khosla, Michael Bernstein, Alexander C. Berg, and Li Fei-Fei. 2015. ImageNet Large Scale Visual Recognition Challenge. *International Journal of Computer Vision (IJCV)*, 115(3):211–252.

Karen Simonyan and Andrew Zisserman. 2014. Two-stream convolutional networks for action recognition in videos. In *Advances in neural information processing systems*, pages 568–576.

Jeffrey Mark Siskind. 1990. Acquiring core meanings of words, represented as jackendoff-style conceptual structures, from correlated streams of linguistic and non-linguistic input. In *Proceedings of the 28th annual meeting on Association for Computational Linguistics*, pages 143–156. Association for Computational Linguistics.

Khurram Soomro, Amir Roshan Zamir, and Mubarak Shah. 2012. Ucf101: A dataset of 101 human actions classes from videos in the wild. *arXiv preprint arXiv:1212.0402*.

Du Tran, Lubomir Bourdev, Rob Fergus, Lorenzo Torresani, and Manohar Paluri. 2015. Learning spatiotemporal features with 3d convolutional networks. In *Proceedings of the IEEE international conference on computer vision*, pages 4489–4497.

Subhashini Venugopalan, Marcus Rohrbach, Jeff Donahue, Raymond Mooney, Trevor Darrell, and Kate Saenko. 2015. Sequence to sequence – video to text. In *Proceedings of the IEEE International Conference on Computer Vision (ICCV)*.

Carl Vondrick, Donald Patterson, and Deva Ramanan. 2013. Efficiently scaling up crowdsourced video annotation. *International Journal of Computer Vision*, 101(1):184–204.

Liwei Wang, Yin Li, and Svetlana Lazebnik. 2016. Learning deep structure-preserving image-text embeddings. In *Proceedings of the IEEE conference on computer vision and pattern recognition*, pages 5005–5013.

Christian Wolf, Eric Lombardi, Julien Mille, Oya Celiktutan, Mingyuan Jiu, Emre Dogan, Gonen Eren, Moez Baccouche, Emmanuel Dellandréa, Charles-Edmond Bichot, et al. 2014. Evaluation of video activity localizations integrating quality and quantity measurements. *Computer Vision and Image Understanding*, 127:14–30.

Masataka Yamaguchi, Kuniaki Saito, Yoshitaka Ushiku, and Tatsuya Harada. 2017. Spatio-temporal person retrieval via natural language queries. *arXiv preprint arXiv:1704.07945*.

Yezhou Yang, Ching Lik Teo, Hal Daumé III, and Yiannis Aloimonos. 2011. Corpus-guided sentence generation of natural images. In *Proceedings of the Conference on Empirical Methods in Natural Language Processing*, pages 444–454. Association for Computational Linguistics.

Xuwang Yin and Vicente Ordonez. 2017. Obj2text: Generating visually descriptive language from object layouts. In *Proceedings of the 2017 Conference on Empirical Methods in Natural Language Processing*, pages 177–187.

Haonan Yu and Jeffrey Mark Siskind. 2013. Grounded language learning from video described with sentences. In *Proceedings of the 51st Annual Meeting of the Association for Computational Linguistics (Volume 1: Long Papers)*, volume 1, pages 53–63.

Licheng Yu, Zhe Lin, Xiaohui Shen, Jimei Yang, Xin Lu, Mohit Bansal, and Tamara L Berg. 2018. Mattnet: Modular attention network for referring expression comprehension. In *Proceedings of the IEEE Conference on Computer Vision and Pattern Recognition (CVPR)*.

Xizhou Zhu, Yujie Wang, Jifeng Dai, Lu Yuan, and Yichen Wei. 2017. Flow-guided feature aggregation for video object detection. In *Proceedings of the IEEE International Conference on Computer Vision*, volume 3.

A Survey on Biomedical Image Captioning

Vasiliki Kougia, John Pavlopoulos, Ion Androutsopoulos
Department of Informatics, Athens University of Economics and Business, Greece
{kouyiav,annis,ion}@aueb.gr

Abstract

Image captioning applied to biomedical images can assist and accelerate the diagnosis process followed by clinicians. This article is the first survey of biomedical image captioning, discussing datasets, evaluation measures, and state of the art methods. Additionally, we suggest two baselines, a weak and a stronger one; the latter outperforms all current state of the art systems on one of the datasets.

1 Introduction

Radiologists or other physicians may need to examine many biomedical images daily, e.g. PET/CT scans or radiology images, and write their findings as medical reports (Figure 1b). Methods assisting physicians to focus on interesting image regions (Shin et al., 2016) or to describe findings (Jing et al., 2018) can reduce medical errors (e.g., suggesting findings to inexperienced physicians) and benefit medical departments by reducing the cost per exam (Bates et al., 2001; Lee et al., 2017).

Despite the importance of biomedical image captioning, related resources are not easily accessible, hindering the emergence of new methods. The publicly available datasets are only three and not always directly available.[1] Also, there is currently no assessment of simple baselines to determine the lower performance boundary and estimate the difficulty of the task. By contrast, complex (typically deep learning) systems are compared to other complex systems, without establishing if they surpass baselines (Zhang et al., 2017b; Wang et al., 2018). Furthermore, current evaluation measures are adopted directly from generic image captioning, ignoring the more challenging nature of the biomedical domain (Cohen

---

(a) General image caption.

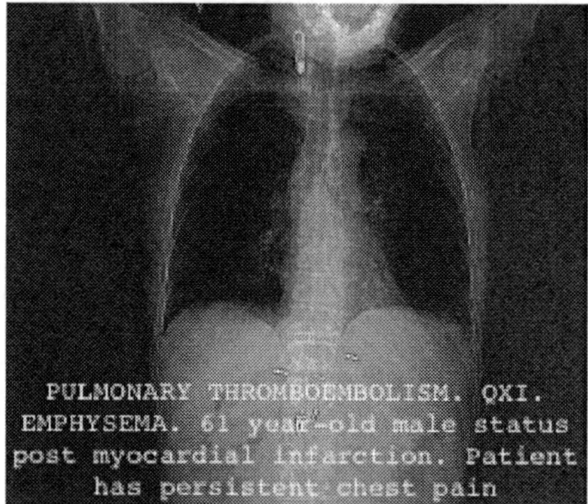

(b) Biomedical image caption.

Figure 1: Example of a caption produced by the model of Vinyals et al. (2015) for a non-biomedical image (1a), and example of a radiology image with its associated caption (1b) from the Pathology Education Informational Resource (PEIR) Digital Library.

and Demner-Fushman, 2014) and thus the potential benefit from employing other measures (Kilickaya et al., 2016). Addressing these limitations is crucial for the fast development of the field.

This paper is the first overview of biomedical image captioning methods, datasets, and evaluation measures. Section 2 describes publicly available datasets. To increase accessibility and ensure consistent results across systems, we provide code to download and preprocess all the datasets. Section 3 describes biomedical image captioning

---

[1] See, for example, http://peir.path.uab.edu/ library/ that requires web scrapping.

Proceedings of the Second Workshop on Shortcomings in Vision and Language, pages 26–36
Minneapolis, USA, June 6, 2019. ©2017 Association for Computational Linguistics

methods and attempts to compare their results, with the caveat that only two works use the same dataset (Shin et al., 2016; Jing et al., 2018) and can be directly compared. Section 4 describes evaluation measures that have been used and introduces two baselines. The first one is based on word frequencies and provides a low performance boundary. The second one is based on image retrieval and the assumption that similar images have similar diagnoses; we show that it is a strong baseline outperforming the state of the art in at least one dataset. Section 7 discusses related (mostly deep learning) biomedical image processing methods for other tasks, such as image classification and segmentation. Section 8 highlights limitations of our work and proposes future directions.

2 Datasets

Datasets for biomedical image captioning comprise medical images and associated texts. Publicly available datasets contain X-rays (IU X-RAY in Table 1), clinical photographs (PEIR GROSS in Table 1), or a mixture of X-rays and photographs (ICLEF-CAPTION in Table 1). The associated texts may be single sentences describing the images, or longer medical reports based on the images (e.g., as in Figure 1b). Current publicly available datasets are rather small (IU X-RAY, PEIR GROSS) or noisy (e.g., IMAGE-CLEF, which is the largest dataset, was created by automatic means that introduced a lot of noise). We do not include in Table 1 datasets like the one of Wang et al. (2017), because their medical reports are not publicly available.[2] Furthermore, we observe that all three publicly available biomedical image captioning datasets suffer from two main shortcomings:

- There is a great class imbalance, with most images having no reported findings.

- The wide range of diseases leads to very scarce occurrences of disease-related terms, making it difficult for models to generalize.

IU X-RAY

Demner-Fushman et al. (2015) presented an approach for developing a collection of radiology examinations, including images and narrative reports by radiologists. The authors suggested an accurate anonymization approach for textual radiology reports and provided public access to their dataset through the Open Access Biomedical Image Search Engine (OpenI).[3] The images are 7,470 frontal and lateral chest X-rays, and each radiology report consists of four sections. The 'comparison' section contains previous information about the patient (e.g., preceding medical exams); the 'indication' section contains symptoms (e.g., hypoxia) or reasons of examination (e.g., age); 'findings' lists the radiology observations; and 'impression' outlines the final diagnosis. A system would ideally generate the 'findings' and 'impression' sections, possibly concatenated (Jing et al., 2018).

The 'impression' and 'findings' sections of the dataset of Demner-Fushman et al. (2015) were used to manually associate each report with a number of tags (called manual encoding), which were Medical Subject Heading (MESH)[4] and RadLex[5] terms assigned by two trained coders. Additionally, each report was associated with automatically extracted tags, produced by Medical Text Indexer[6] (called MTI encoding). These tags allow systems to learn to initially generate terms describing the image and then use the image along with the generated terms to produce the caption. Hence, this dataset, which is the only one in the field with manually annotated tags, has an added value. From our processing, we found that 104 reports contained no image, 489 were missing 'findings', 6 were missing 'impression', and 25 were missing both 'findings' and 'impression'; the 40 image-caption-tags triplets corresponding to the latter 25 reports were discarded in our later experiments. We shuffled the instances of the dataset (image-text-tags triplets) and used 6,674 of them as the training set (images from the 90% of the reports), with average caption length 38 words and vocabulary size 2,091. Only 2,745 training captions were unique, because 59% of them were the same in more than one image (e.g., similar images with the same condition). Table 1 provides more information about the datasets and their splits.

PEIR GROSS

The Pathology Education Informational Resource (PEIR) digital library is a public access image

---

[2]See, for example, also https://nihcc.app.box.com/v/ChestXray-NIHCC where only images and text-mined disease labels are released for public use.

[3]https://openi.nlm.nih.gov/
[4] https://goo.gl/iDvwj2
[5]http://www.radlex.org/
[6]https://ii.nlm.nih.gov/MTI/

Dataset	Images	Tags	Texts
IU X-RAY	7,470 X-rays	MESH & MTI extracted terms	3,955 reports
PEIR GROSS	7,443 teaching images	top TF-IDF caption words	7,443 sentences
ICLEF-CAPTION	232,305 medical images	UMLS concepts	232,305 sentences

Dataset	Training Instances	Test Instances	Total
IU X-RAY	6,674	756	7,430
PEIR GROSS	6,698	745	7,443
ICLEF-CAPTION	200,074	22,231	232,305

Table 1: Biomedical image captioning publicly available datasets. Images are annotated with tags, which may be medical terms (IU X-RAY) or words from the captions (PEIR GROSS) (Jing et al., 2018). A text may be linked to a single image (PEIR GROSS & ICLEF-CAPTION) or multiple ones (IU X-RAY). It may comprise a single sentence (PEIR GROSS) or multiple sentences (ICLEF-CAPTION, IU X-RAY). The lower table shows the number of training and test instances (image-text-tags triples) in each dataset, as used in our experiments. We excluded 40 out of the 7,470 IU X-RAY instances, as discussed in the main text.

database for use in medical education.[7] Jing et al. (2018), who were the first to use images from this database, employed 7,442 teaching images of gross lesions (i.e., visible to the naked eye) from 21 PEIR pathology sub-categories, along with their associated captions.[8] We developed code that downloads the images for this dataset (called PEIR GROSS) and preprocesses their respective captions, which we release for public use.[9]

The dataset is split to 6,698 train and 745 test instances (Table 1).[10] The vocabulary size from the train captions is 4,051 with average caption length 17 words. From the 6,698 train captions only 632 were duplicates (i.e., the same caption for more than one images), which explains why this dataset has a much larger vocabulary than IU X-RAY, despite the fact that captions are shorter.

ICLEF-CAPTION

This dataset was released in 2017 for the Image Concept Detection and Caption Prediction (ICLEF-CAPTION) task (Eickhoff et al., 2017) of IMAGE-CLEF (de Herrera et al., 2018). The dataset consists of 184,614 biomedical images and their captions, extracted from biomedical articles on PubMed Central (PMC).[11] The organizers used an automatic method, based on a biomedical image type hierarchy (Müller et al., 2012), to classify the 5.8M extracted images as clinical or not and also discard compound ones (e.g., images consisting of multiple X-rays), but their estimation was that the overall noise in the dataset would be as high as 10% or 20% (Eickhoff et al., 2017).

In 2018, the ICLEF-CAPTION organizers employed a Convolutional Neural Network (CNN), to classify the same 5.8M images based on their type and to extract the non-compound clinical ones, leading to 232,305 images along with their respective captions (de Herrera et al., 2018). Although they reported that compound images were reduced, they noted that noise still exists, with non-clinical images present (e.g., images of maps). Additionally, a wide diversity between the types of the images has been reported (Liang et al., 2017). The length of the captions varies from 1 to 816 words (Su et al., 2018; Liang et al., 2017). Only 1.4% of the captions are duplicates (associated with more than one image), probably due to the wide image type diversity. The average caption length is 21 words and the vocabulary size is 157,256. A further 10k instances were used for testing in 2018, but they are not publicly available. Hence, in our experiments we split the 235,305 instances into training and test subsets (Table 1).

For tag annotation, the organizers used QUICK-UMLS (Soldaini and Goharian, 2016) to identify concepts of the Unified Medical Language System (UMLS) in the caption text, extracting 111,155 unique concepts from the 222,305 captions. Each image is linked to 30 UMLS concepts, on average, while fewer than 6k have one or two asso-

---

[7] http://peir.path.uab.edu/library/

[8] PEIR pathology contains 23 sub-categories, but only 22 contain a gross sub-collection (7,443 images in total). We observe that one image was not included by Jing et al. (2018).

[9] Our code is publicly available at https://github.com/nlpaueb/bio_image_caption.

[10] We used 10% of the dataset for testing, as the 1k images used by Jing et al. for validation and testing were not released.

[11] https://www.ncbi.nlm.nih.gov/pmc/

ciated concepts and there are images associated with even thousands of concepts. The organizers observe the existence of noise and note that irrelevant concepts have been extracted, mainly due to the fully automatic extraction process.

3 Methods

Varges et al. (2012) employed Natural Language Generation to assist medical professionals turn cardiological findings (e.g., from diagnostic imaging procedures) into fluent and readable textual descriptions. From a different perspective, Schlegl et al. (2015) used both the image and the textual report as input to a CNN, trained to classify images with the help of automatically extracted semantic concepts from the textual report. Kisilev et al. (2015a,b) employed a radiologist to mark an image lesion, and a semi-automatic segmentation approach to define the boundaries of that lesion. Then, they used structured Support Vector Machines (Tsochantaridis et al., 2004) to generate semantic tags, originating from a radiology lexicon, for each lesion. In subsequent work they used a CNN to rank suspicious regions of diagnostic images and, then, generate tags for the top ranked regions, which can be embedded in diagnostic sentence templates (Kisilev et al., 2016).

Shin et al. (2016) were the first to apply a CNN-RNN encoder-decoder approach to generate captions from medical images. They used the IU X-RAY dataset and a Network in Network (Lin et al., 2013) or GoogLeNet (Szegedy et al., 2015) as the encoder of the images, obtaining better results with GoogLeNet. The encoder was pretrained to predict (from the images) 17 classes, corresponding to MESH terms that were frequent in the reports and did not co-occur frequently with other MESH terms. An LSTM (Hochreiter and Schmidhuber, 1997) or GRU (Cho et al., 2014) was used as the RNN decoder to generate image descriptions from the image encodings. In a second training phase, the mean of the RNNs state vectors (obtained while describing each image) was used as an improved representation of each training image. The original 17 classes that had been used to pretrain the CNN were replaced by 57 finer classes, by applying k-means clustering to the improved vector representations of the training images. The CNN was then retrained to predict the 57 new classes and this led to improved BLEU (Papineni et al., 2002) scores for the overall CNN-RNN system. The gen-

erated descriptions, however, were not evaluated by humans. Furthermore, the generated descriptions were up to 5 words long and looked more like bags of terms (e.g., 'aorta thoracic, tortuous, mild'), rather than fluent coherent reports.

Zhang et al. (2017b) were the first to employ an attention mechanism in biomedical image to text generation, with their MDNET.[12] MDNET used RESNET (He et al., 2016) for image encoding, but extending its skip connections to address vanishing gradients. The image representation acts as the starting hidden state of a decoder LSTM, enhanced with an attention mechanism over the image. (During training, this attention mechanism is also employed to detect diagnostic labels.) The decoder is cloned to generate a fixed number of sentences, as many as the symptom descriptions. This model performed slightly better than a state of the art generic image captioning model (Karpathy and Fei-Fei, 2015) in most evaluation measures.

Jing et al. (2018) segment each image to equally sized patches and use VGG-19 (Simonyan and Zisserman, 2014) to separately encode each patch as a 'visual' feature vector. A Multi-Layer Perceptron (MLP) is then fed with the visual feature vectors of each image (representing its patches) and predicts terms from a pre-determined term vocabulary. The word embeddings of the predicted terms of each image are treated as 'semantic' feature vectors representing the image. The decoder, which produces the image description, is a hierarchical RNN, consisting of a sentence-level LSTM and a word-level LSTM. The sentence-level LSTM produces a sequence of embeddings, each specifying the information to be expressed by a sentence of the image description (acting as a topic). For each sentence embedding, the word-level LSTM then produces the words of the corresponding sentence, word by word. More precisely, at each one of its time-steps, the sentence-level LSTM of Jing et al. examines both the visual and the semantic feature vectors of the image. Following previous work on image captioning, that added attention to encoder-decoder approaches (Xu et al., 2015; You et al., 2016; Zhang et al., 2017b), an attention mechanism (an MLP fed with the current state of the sentence-level

---

[12]Zhang et al. had introduced earlier TandemNet (Zhang et al., 2017a), which also used attention, but for biomedical image classification. TandemNet could perform captioning, but the authors considered this task as future work, that was addressed with MDNET.

LSTM and each one of the visual feature vectors of the image) assigns attention scores to the visual feature vectors, and the weighted sum of the visual feature vectors (weighted by their attention scores) becomes a visual 'context' vector, specifying which patches of the image to express by the next sentence. Another attention mechanism (another MLP) assigns attention scores to the semantic feature vectors (that represent the terms of the image), and the weighted sum of the semantic feature vectors (weighted by attention) becomes the semantic context vector, specifying which terms of the image to express by the next sentence. At each time-step, the sentence-level LSTM considers the visual and semantic context vectors, produces a sentence embedding and updates its state, until a stop control instructs it to stop. Given the sentence embedding, the word-level LSTM produces the words of the corresponding sentence, again until a special 'stop' token is generated. Jing et al. showed that their model outperforms models created for general image captioning with visual attention (Vinyals et al., 2015; Donahue et al., 2015; Xu et al., 2015; You et al., 2016).

Wang et al. (2018) adopted an approach similar to that of Jing et al. (2018), using a RESNET-based CNN to encode the images and an LSTM decoder to produce image descriptions, but their LSTM is flat, as opposed to the hierarchical LSTM of Jing et al. (2018). Wang et al. also demonstrated that it is possible to extract additional image features from the states of the LSTM, much as Jing et al. (2018), but using a more elaborate attention-based mechanism, combining textual and visual information. Wang et al. experimented with the same OpenI dataset that Shin et al. and Jing et al. used. However, they did not provide evaluation results on OpenI and, hence, no direct comparison can be made against the results of Shin et al. and Jing et al. Nevertheless, focusing on experiments that generated paragraph-sized image descriptions, the results of Wang et al. on the (not publicly available) CHEST X-RAY dataset (e.g., BLEU-1 0.2860, BLEU-2 0.1597) are much worse than the OpenI results of Jing et al. (e.g., BLEU-1 0.517, BLEU-2 0.386), possibly because of the flat (not hierarchical) LSTM decoder of Wang et al.[13]

ICLEF-CAPTION run successfully for two consecutive years (Eickhoff et al., 2017; de Herrera et al., 2018) and stopped in 2019. Participating systems (see Table 3) used image similarity to retrieve images similar to the one to be described, then aggregating the captions of the retrieved images; or they employed an encoder-decoder architecture; or they simply classified each image based on UMLS concepts and then aggregated the respective UMLS 'semantic groups'[14] to form a caption. Liang et al. (2017) used a pre-trained VG-GNET CNN encoder and an LSTM decoder, similarly to Karpathy and Fei-Fei (2015). They trained three such models on different caption lengths and used an SVM classifier to choose the most suitable decoder for the given image. Furthermore, they used a 1-Nearest Neighbor method to retrieve the caption of the most similar image and aggregated it with the generated caption. Zhang et al. (2018), who achieved the best results in 2018, used the Lucene Image Retrieval software (LIRE) to retrieve images from the training set and then simply concatenated the captions of the top three retrieved images to obtain the new caption. Abacha et al. (2017) used GoogLeNet to detect UMLS concepts and returned the aggregation of their respective UMLS semantic groups as a caption. Su et al. (2018) and Rahman (2018) also employed different encoder-decoder architectures.

Gale et al. (2018) argued that existing biomedical image captioning systems fail to produce a satisfactory medical diagnostic report from an image, and to provide evidence for a medical decision. They focused on classifying hip fractures in pelvic X-rays, and argued that the diagnostic report of such narrow medical tasks could be simplified to two sentence templates; one for positive cases, including 5 placeholders to be filled by descriptive terms, and a fixed negative one. They used DENSENET (Huang et al., 2017) to get image embeddings and a two-layer LSTM, with attention over the image, to generate the constrained textual report. Their results, shown in Table 2, are very high, but this is expected due to the extremely simplified and standardized ground truth reports. (Gale et al. report an improvement of more than 50 BLEU points when employing this assumption.) The reader is also warned that the results of Table 2 are not directly comparable, since they are obtained from very different datasets.

---

[13]CHEST X-RAY 14 contains 112,120 X-ray images with tags (14 disease labels) and medical reports, but only the images and tags (not the reports) are publicly available.

[14]https://goo.gl/GFbx1d

Method	Dataset	B1	B2	B3	B4	MET	ROU	CID
Shin et al. (2016)	IU X-RAY	78.5	14.4	4.7	0.0	-	-	-
Jing et al. (2018)	IU X-RAY	51.7	38.6	30.6	24.7	21.7	44.7	32.7
	PEIR GROSS	30.0	21.8	16.5	11.3	14.9	27.9	32.9
Wang et al. (2018)	CHEST X-RAY 14†	28.6	15.9	10.3	7.3	10.7	22.6	-
Zhang et al. (2017b)	BCIDR†	91.2	82.9	75.0	67.7	39.6	70.1	2.04
Gale et al. (2018)	FRONTAL PELVIC X-RAYS†	91.9	83.8	76.1	67.7	-	-	-

Table 2: Evaluation of biomedical image captioning methods with BLEU-1/-2/-3/-4 (B1, B2, B3, B4), METEOR (MET), ROUGE-L (ROU), and CIDER (CID) percentage scores. Zhang et al. (2017a) and Han et al. (2018) also performed biomedical captioning, but did not provide any evaluation results. Datasets with † are not publicly available; BDIDR consists of 1,000 pathological bladder cancer images, each with 5 reports; FRONTAL PELVIC X-RAYS comprises 50,363 images, each supplemented with a radiology report, but simplified to a standard template; CHEST X-RAY 14 is publicly available, but without its medical reports.

Team	Year	Approach	BLEU
Liang et al.	2017	ED+IR	26.00
Zhang et al.	2018	IR	25.01
Abacha et al.	2017	CLS	22.47
Su et al.	2018	ED	17.99
Rahman	2018	ED	17.25

Table 3: Top-5 participating systems at the ICLEF-CAPTION competition, ranked based on average BLEU (%), the official evaluation measure. Systems used an encoder-decoder (ED), image retrieval (IR), or classified UMLS concepts (CLS). We exclude 2017 systems employing external resources, which may have seen test data during training (Eickhoff et al., 2017). 2018 models were limited to use only pre-trained CNNs.

4 Evaluation

The most common evaluation measures in biomedical image captioning are BLEU (Papineni et al., 2002), ROUGE (Lin, 2004) and METEOR (Banerjee and Lavie, 2005), which originate from machine translation and summarization. The more recent CIDER measure (Vedantam et al., 2015), which was designed for general image captioning (Kilickaya et al., 2016), has been used in only two biomedical image captioning works (Zhang et al., 2017b; Jing et al., 2018). SPICE (Anderson et al., 2016), which was also designed for general image captioning (Kilickaya et al., 2016), has not been used in any biomedical image captioning work we are aware of. Below, we describe each measure separately and discuss its advantages and limitations with respect to biomedical image captioning.

BLEU is the most common measure (Papineni et al., 2002). It measures word n-gram overlap between the generated and the ground truth caption.

A brevity penalty is added to penalize short generated captions. BLEU-1 considers unigrams (i.e., words), while BLEU-2, -3, -4 consider bigrams, trigrams, and 4-grams respectively. The average of the four variants was used as the official measure in ICLEF-CAPTION.

METEOR (Banerjee and Lavie, 2005) extended BLEU-1 by employing the harmonic mean of precision and recall (F-score), biased towards recall, and by also employing stemming (Porter stemmer) and synonymy (WordNet). To take into account longer subsequences, it includes a penalty of up to 50% when no common n-grams exist between the machine-generated description and the reference.

ROUGE-L (Lin et al., 2013) is the ratio of the length of the longest common subsequence between the machine-generated description and the reference human description, to the size of the reference (ROUGE-L recall); or to the generated description (ROUGE-L precision); or a combination of the two (ROUGE-L F-measure). We note that several ROUGE variants exist, based on different n-gram lengths, stemming, stopword removal, etc., but ROUGE-L is the most commonly used variant in biomedical image captioning so far.

CIDER (Vedantam et al., 2015) measures the cosine similarity between n-gram TF-IDF representations of the two captions (words are also stemmed). This is calculated for unigrams to 4-grams and their average is returned as the final evaluation score. The intuition behind using TF-IDF is to reward frequent caption terms while penalizing common ones (e.g., stopwords). However, biomedical image captioning datasets contain many scientific terms (e.g., disease names) that are common across captions (or more generally document collections), which may be mistakenly penalized. We also noticed that the scores returned by the provided CIDER implementation may exceed 100%.[15] We exclude CIDER results, since these issues need to be investigated further.

SPICE (Anderson et al., 2016) extracts tuples from the two captions (machine-generated, reference), containing objects, attributes and/or relations; e.g., (patient), (has, pain), (male, patient). Precision and recall are computed using WordNet synonym matching between the two sets of tuples, and the F1 score is returned. The creators of SPICE report improved results over both METEOR and CIDER, but it has been noted that results depend on parsing quality (Kilickaya et al., 2016). When experimenting with the provided implementation[16] of this measure, we noticed that it failed to parse long texts to evaluate them. Similarly to CIDER, we exclude SPICE from further analysis below.

Word Mover's Distance (WMD) (Kusner et al., 2015) computes the minimum cumulative cost required to move all word embeddings of one caption to aligned word embeddings of the other caption.[17] It completely ignores, however, word order, and thus readability, which is one of the main assessment dimensions in the biomedical field (Tsatsaronis et al., 2015). Other previously discussed n-gram based measures also largely ignore word order, but at least consider local order (inside n-grams). WMD scores are included in Table 4 as similarity values $\text{WMS} = (1 + \text{WMD})^{-1}$.

5 Baselines

5.1 Frequency Baseline

The first baseline we propose (FREQUENCY) uses the frequency of words in the training captions to always generate the same caption. The most frequent word always becomes the first word of the caption, the next most frequent word always becomes the second word of the caption, etc. The number of words in the generated caption is the average length of training captions. Systems should at least outperform this simplistic baseline and its score should be low across datasets.

5.2 Nearest Neighbor Baseline

The second baseline (NEAREST-NEIGHBOR) is based on the intuition that similar biomedical images have similar diagnostic captions; this would also explain why image retrieval systems perform well in biomedical image captioning (Table 3). We use RESNET-18[18] to encode images, and cosine similarity to retrieve similar training images. The caption of the most similar retrieved image is returned as the generated caption of a new image. This baseline can be improved by employing an image encoder trained on biomedical images, such as X-rays (Rajpurkar et al., 2017).

6 Experimental Results

As shown in Table 4, FREQUENCY scores high when evaluated with BLEU-1 and WMS, probably because these measures are based on unigrams. FREQUENCY, which simply concatenates the most common words of the training captions, is rewarded every time the most common words appear in the reference captions.

To our surprise, NEAREST-NEIGHBOR outperforms not only FREQUENCY, but also the state of the art in PEIR GROSS, in all evaluation measures (Table 4). This could be explained by the fact that PEIR GROSS images are phototographs of medical conditions, not X-rays, and thus they may be handled better by the RESNET-18 encoder of NEAREST-NEIGHBOR. In future work, we intend to experiment with an encoder trained on medical images (e.g., CHEXNET).[19]

In IU X-RAY, NEAREST-NEIGHBOR scores low in all measures, possibly because in this case the images are X-rays and the RESNET-18 encoder fails to handle them properly. Again, by experimenting with a different encoder, trained on X-rays, this baseline might be improved.

In ICLEF-CAPTION, both of our baselines perform poorly, and much worse than the best system (cf. Table 3), which achieved average BLEU 26%. This is partially explained by the size of this dataset (Section 2), which contains multiple different images and captions. Moreover, this dataset was created automatically and includes noise and a great diversity of image types (e.g., irrelevant, generic images such as maps) and captions.

---

[15]We used the official evaluation server implementation CIDER-D (Chen et al., 2015).

[16]https://goo.gl/bo11Bz

[17]We used Gensim's implementation of WMD (https://goo.gl/epzecP) and biomedical word2vec embeddings (https://archive.org/details/pubmed2018_w2v_200D.tar).

[18]https://goo.gl/28K1y2

[19]https://stanfordmlgroup.github.io/projects/chexnet/

Dataset	Baseline	B1	B2	B3	B4	MET	ROU	WMS
PEIR GROSS	FREQUENCY	29.4	6.9	0.0	0.0	12.2	17.9	23.6
	NEAREST-NEIGHBOR	**34.6**	**26.2**	**20.6**	**15.6**	**18.1**	**34.7**	**27.5**
	State of the art	30.0	21.8	16.5	11.3	14.9	27.9	–
IU X-RAY	FREQUENCY	44.2	7.8	0.0	0.0	17.6	18.7	**30.2**
	NEAREST-NEIGHBOR	28.1	15.2	9.1	5.7	12.5	20.9	26.0
	State of the art	**78.5**	**38.6**	**30.6**	**24.7**	**21.7**	**44.7**	–
ICLEF-CAPTION	FREQUENCY	**18.2**	1.9	0.1	0.0	**4.6**	**11.1**	**22.1**
	NEAREST-NEIGHBOR	7.5	**3.0**	**1.7**	**1.2**	4.1	8.6	20.7
	State of the art	26.00				–	–	–

Table 4: Evaluation of FREQUENCY and NEAREST-NEIGHBOR on all datasets, with BLEU-1/-2/-3/-4 (B1, B2, B3, B4), METEOR (MET), ROUGE (ROU), Word Mover's Similarity (WMS) percent scores. Best results to date per dataset are also included (state of the art). In ICLEF-CAPTION, only the average BLEU has been reported (26.00).

7 Related Fields

Deep learning methods have been widely applied to biomedical images and address various biomedical imaging tasks (Litjens et al., 2017). Below, we briefly describe the tasks that are most related to biomedical image captioning, namely biomedical image classification, detection, segmentation, retrieval, as well as general image captioning.

The most related field is image captioning for general images. This is not a new task (Duygulu et al., 2002), but recent work leverages big datasets and has achieved impressive results on generating natural language captions (Karpathy and Fei-Fei, 2015). The work of Xu et al. (2015) was the first to incorporate attention to the encoder-decoder architecture for image captioning. Appart from improving performance, attention over images helps visualize how the model decides to generate each word and improves interpretability. Image captioning can also be addressed jointly with other tasks, such as video captioning (Donahue et al., 2015) or image tagging (Shin et al., 2016).

Biomedical image classification aims at classifying a biomedical image as normal or abnormal, or assigning multiple disease labels (Rajpurkar et al., 2017, 2018). Also, it may refer to classifying an abnormality as malignant or benign (Esteva et al., 2017), or assigning other labels (e.g, labels showing the severity of a lesion). A related task is biomedical image detection, which is used to localize and highlight organs or wider anatomical regions (de Vos et al., 2016) as well as specific abnormalities (Dou et al., 2016). This task is performed as a first step to assist other tasks, such as image classification or segmentation (Bi et al.,

2017; Rajpurkar et al., 2017).

Biomedical image segmentation aims to divide a biomedical image to different regions representing organs or abnormalities, which can be used for further medical analysis, to learn their features, or classification. The most popular CNN-based architecture is U-NET (Ronneberger et al., 2015), a version of the network of Long et al. (2015), altered to produce more precise outputs. Later works (Ö. Çiçek et al., 2016; Milletari et al., 2016) extended U-NET for 3D image segmentation.

Biomedical image retrieval facilitates searching images in large biomedical databases, based on certain features like symptoms, diseases, and medical cases in general (Liu et al., 2016). Related tasks are also image registration, which performs a spatial alignment of the images (Miao et al., 2016; Yang et al., 2016), biomedical image generation (Bahrami et al., 2016), and resolution enhancement of 2D and 3D biomedical images (Oktay et al., 2016).

8 Limitations and Future Work

This paper is a first step towards a more extensive survey of biomedical image captioning methods. We plan to improve it in several ways. Firstly, we hope to investigate to a larger extent the differences between generic image captioning and biomedical image captioning. For example, generic image captioning aims to describe an image, whereas biomedical captioning should ideally help in diagnosis; parts of the image with no diagnostic interest are typically not discussed in a medical report. This investigation may also shed more light to the discussion of appropriate evaluation measures for biomedical image captioning, and the extent to which evaluation measures from generic image captioning, summarizaton, or machine translation are appropriate.

Secondly, we hope to distill key features from current biomedical image captioning methods (e.g., methods that first tag the images and then generate captions from both the images and their tags vs. methods that directly generate captions; methods that retrieve similar images vs. methods that do not; types of pretraining used in image encoders and text decoders). This will allow us to provide a more structured and coherent presentation of current methods and highlight possible choices that have not been explored so far.

Thirdly, we plan to consult physicians (e.g., radiologists, nuclear doctors) to obtain a better view of their real-life needs and the degree to which current methods are aligned with their needs. We would also like to contribute to a roadmap of future activities towards integrating biomedical image captioning methods in real-life diagnostic procedures and clinical diagnosis systems.

Acknowledgments

We are grateful to the anonymous reviewers, who suggested several of the future possible improvements mentioned above. We also thank Dr. Dimitrios Papamichail for discussions that motivated us to consider biomedical image captioning.

References

A. B. Abacha, A. García Seco de Herrera, S. Gayen, D. Demner-Fushman, and S. Antani. 2017. NLM at ImageCLEF 2017 caption task. In *CLEF CEUR Workshop*, Dublin, Ireland.

P. Anderson, B. Fernando, M. Johnson, and S. Gould. 2016. SPICE: Semantic propositional image caption evaluation. In *ECCV*, pages 382–398, Amsterdam, Netherlands.

K. Bahrami, F. Shi, I. Rekik, and D. Shen. 2016. Convolutional neural network for reconstruction of 7T-like images from 3T MRI using appearance and anatomical features. In *Deep Learning and Data Labeling for Medical Applications*, pages 39–47, Athens, Greece.

S. Banerjee and A. Lavie. 2005. METEOR: An automatic metric for MT evaluation with improved correlation with human judgments. In *ACL Workshop on Intrinsic and Extrinsic Evaluation Measures for Machine Translation and/or Summarization*, pages 65–72, Ann Arbor, MI, USA.

D. W. Bates, M. Cohen, L. L. Leape, J. M. Overhage, M. M. Shabot, and T. Sheridan. 2001. Reducing the frequency of errors in medicine using information technology. *Journal of the American Medical Informatics Association*, 8(4):299–308.

L. Bi, J. Kim, A. Kumar, L. Wen, D. Feng, and M. Fulham. 2017. Automatic detection and classification of regions of FDG uptake in whole-body PET-CT lymphoma studies. *Computerized Medical Imaging and Graphics*, 60:3–10.

X. Chen, H. Fang, T.-Y. Lin, R. Vedantam, S. Gupta, P. Dollr, and C. L. Zitnick. 2015. Microsoft COCO captions: Data collection and evaluation server. *arXiv:1504.00325*.

K. Cho, B. van Merrienboer, C. Gulcehre, D. Bahdanau, F. Bougares, H. Schwenk, and Y. Bengio. 2014. Learning phrase representations using RNN encoder–decoder for statistical machine translation. In *EMNLP*, pages 1724–1734, Doha, Qatar.

K. B. Cohen and D. Demner-Fushman. 2014. *Biomedical Natural Language Processing*. John Benjamins.

D. Demner-Fushman, M. D. Kohli, M. B. Rosenman, S. E. Shooshan, L. Rodriguez, S. Antani, G. R. Thoma, and C. J. McDonald. 2015. Preparing a collection of radiology examinations for distribution and retrieval. *Journal of the American Medical Informatics Association*, 23(2):304–310.

J. Donahue, L. Anne Hendricks, S. Guadarrama, M. Rohrbach, S. Venugopalan, K. Saenko, and T. Darrell. 2015. Long-term recurrent convolutional networks for visual recognition and description. In *CVPR*, pages 2625–2634, Boston, MA, USA.

Q. Dou, H. Chen, L. Yu, L. Zhao, J. Qin, D. Wang, V. CT. Mok, L. Shi, and P.-A. Heng. 2016. Automatic detection of cerebral microbleeds from MR images via 3D convolutional neural networks. *IEEE Transactions on Medical Imaging*, 35(5):1182–1195.

P. Duygulu, K. Barnard, J. F. G. de Freitas, and D. A. Forsyth. 2002. Object recognition as machine translation: Learning a lexicon for a fixed image vocabulary. In *ECCV*, pages 97–112, Florence, Italy.

C. Eickhoff, I. Schwall, A. García Seco de Herrera, and H. Müller. 2017. Overview of ImageCLEFcaption 2017 - Image caption prediction and concept extraction tasks to understand biomedical images. In *CLEF CEUR Workshop*, Dublin, Ireland.

A. Esteva, B. Kuprel, R. A. Novoa, J. Ko, S. M. Swetter, H. M. Blau, and S. Thrun. 2017. Dermatologist-level classification of skin cancer with deep neural networks. *Nature*, 542(7639):115–118.

W. Gale, L. Oakden-Rayner, G. Carneiro, A. P. Bradley, and L. J. Palmer. 2018. Producing radiologist-quality reports for interpretable articial intelligence. *arXiv:1806.00340*.

Z. Han, B. Wei, S. Leung, J. Chung, and S. Li. 2018. Towards automatic report generation in spine radiology using weakly supervised framework. In *International Conference on Medical Image Computing and Computer-Assisted Intervention*, pages 185–193, Granada, Spain.

K. He, X. Zhang, S. Ren, and J. Sun. 2016. Deep residual learning for image recognition. In *CVPR*, pages 770–778, Las Vegas, USA.

A. García Seco de Herrera, C. Eickhoff, V. Andrearczyk, and H. Müller. 2018. Overview of the ImageCLEF 2018 caption prediction tasks. In *CLEF CEUR Workshop*, Avignon, France.

S. Hochreiter and J. Schmidhuber. 1997. Long short-term memory. *Neural Computation*, 9(8):1735–1780.

G. Huang, Z. Liu, L. Van Der Maaten, and K. Q. Weinberger. 2017. Densely connected convolutional networks. In *CVPR*, pages 4700–4708, Hawaii, HI, USA.

B. Jing, P. Xie, and E. Xing. 2018. On the automatic generation of medical imaging reports. In *ACL*, pages 2577–2586, Melbourne, Australia.

A. Karpathy and L. Fei-Fei. 2015. Deep visual-semantic alignments for generating image descriptions. In *CVPR*, pages 3128–3137, Boston, MA, USA.

M. Kilickaya, A. Erdem, N. Ikizler-Cinbis, and E. Erdem. 2016. Re-evaluating automatic metrics for image captioning. In *EACL*, pages 199–209, Valencia, Spain.

P. Kisilev, E. Sason, E. Barkan, and S. Hashoul. 2016. Medical image captioning: Learning to describe medical image findings using multi-task-loss CNN. In *Deep Learning for Precision Medicine*, Riva del Garda, Italy.

P. Kisilev, E. Walach, E. Barkan, B. Ophir, S. Alpert, and S. Y. Hashoul. 2015a. From medical image to automatic medical report generation. *IBM Journal of Research and Development*, 59(2):1–7.

P. Kisilev, E. Walach, S. Y. Hashoul, E. Barkan, B. Ophir, and S. Alpert. 2015b. Semantic description of medical image findings: Structured learning approach. In *British Machine Vision Conference*, pages 1–11, Swansea, UK.

M. Kusner, Y. Sun, N. Kolkin, and K. Weinberger. 2015. From word embeddings to document distances. In *ICML*, pages 957–966, Lille, France.

J.-G. Lee, S. Jun, Y.-W. Cho, H. Lee, G. B. Kim, J. B. Seo, and N. Kim. 2017. Deep learning in medical imaging: General overview. *Korean Journal of Radiology*, 18(4):570–584.

S. Liang, X. Li, Y. Zhu, X. Li, and S. Jiang. 2017. ISIA at the ImageCLEF 2017 image caption task. In *CLEF CEUR Workshop*, Dublin, Ireland.

C.-Y. Lin. 2004. ROUGE: A package for automatic evaluation of summaries. In *Text Summarization Branches Out ACL Workshop*, pages 74–81, Barcelona, Spain.

M. Lin, Q. Chen, and S. Yan. 2013. Network in network. *arXiv:1312.4400*.

G. Litjens, T. Kooi, B. E. Bejnordi, A. A. A. Setio, F. Ciompi, M. Ghafoorian, J. A.W.M. Van Der Laak, B. Van Ginneken, and C. I. Sánchez. 2017. A survey on deep learning in medical image analysis. *Medical Image Analysis*, 42:60–88.

X. Liu, H. R. Tizhoosh, and J. Kofman. 2016. Generating binary tags for fast medical image retrieval based on convolutional nets and radon transform. In *IJCNN*, pages 2872–2878, Vancouver, Canada.

J. Long, E. Shelhamer, and T. Darrell. 2015. Fully convolutional networks for semantic segmentation. In *CVPR*, pages 3431–3440, Boston, MA, USA.

S. Miao, Z. J. Wang, and R. Liao. 2016. A CNN regression approach for real-time 2D/3D registration. *IEEE transactions on medical imaging*, 35(5):1352–1363.

F. Milletari, N. Navab, and S. Ahmadi. 2016. V-Net: Fully convolutional neural networks for volumetric medical image segmentation. In *International Conference on 3D Vision (3DV)*, pages 565–571, California, CA, USA.

H. Müller, J. Kalpathy-Cramer, D. Demner-Fushman, and S. Antani. 2012. Creating a classification of image types in the medical literature for visual categorization. In *Medical Imaging 2012: Advanced PACS-based Imaging Informatics and Therapeutic Applications*, San Diego, CA, USA.

Ö. Çiçek, A. Abdulkadir, S. S. Lienkamp, T. Brox, and O. Ronneberger. 2016. 3D U-Net: Learning dense volumetric segmentation from sparse annotation. In *Medical Image Computing and Computer-Assisted Intervention*, pages 424–432, Athens, Greece.

O. Oktay, W. Bai, M. Lee, R. Guerrero, K. Kamnitsas, J. Caballero, A. de Marvao, S. Cook, D. ORegan, and D. Rueckert. 2016. Multi-input cardiac image super-resolution using convolutional neural networks. In *International Conference on Medical Image Computing and Computer-Assisted Intervention*, pages 246–254, Athens, Greece.

K. Papineni, S. Roukos, T. Ward, and W.-J. Zhu. 2002. BLEU: A method for automatic evaluation of machine translation. In *ACL*, pages 311–318, Philadelphia, PA, USA.

Md M. Rahman. 2018. A cross modal deep learning based approach for caption prediction and concept detection by CS Morgan State. In *CLEF CEUR Workshop*, Avignon, France.

P. Rajpurkar, J. Irvin, R. L. Ball, K. Zhu, B. Yang, H. Mehta, et al. 2018. Deep learning for chest radiograph diagnosis: A retrospective comparison of the CheXNeXt algorithm to practicing radiologists. *PLOS Medicine*, 15(11):1–17.

P. Rajpurkar, J. Irvin, K. Zhu, B. Yang, H. Mehta, et al. 2017. CheXNet: Radiologist-level pneumonia detection on chestX-rays with deep learning. *arXiv:1711.05225*.

O. Ronneberger, P. Fischer, and T. Brox. 2015. U-Net: Convolutional networks for biomedical image segmentation. In *Medical Image Computing and Computer-Assisted Intervention*, pages 234–241, Munich, Germany.

T. Schlegl, S. M. Waldstein, W.-D. Vogl, U. Schmidt-Erfurth, and G. Langs. 2015. Predicting semantic descriptions from medical images with convolutional neural networks. In *Information Processing in Medical Imaging*, pages 437–448, Isle of Skye, UK.

H.-C. Shin, K. Roberts, L. Lu, D. Demner-Fushman, J. Yao, and R. M. Summers. 2016. Learning to read chest X-rays: Recurrent neural cascade model for automated image annotation. In *CVPR*, pages 2497–2506, Las Vegas, USA.

K. Simonyan and A. Zisserman. 2014. Very deep convolutional networks for large-scale image recognition. *arXiv:1409.1556*.

L. Soldaini and N. Goharian. 2016. QuickUMLS: a fast, unsupervised approach for medical concept extraction. In *MedIR*.

Y. Su, F. Liu, and M. P. Rosen. 2018. UMass at ImageCLEF caption prediction 2018 task. In *CLEF CEUR Workshop*, Avignon, France.

C. Szegedy, W. Liu, Y. Jia, P. Sermanet, S. Reed, D. Anguelov, D. Erhan, V. Vanhoucke, and A. Rabinovich. 2015. Going deeper with convolutions. In *CCVPR*, pages 1–9, Boston, MA, USA.

G. Tsatsaronis, G. Balikas, P. Malakasiotis, I. Partalas, M. Zschunke, M. R. Alvers, D. Weissenborn, A. Krithara, S. Petridis, D. Polychronopoulos, et al. 2015. An overview of the BIOASQ large-scale biomedical semantic indexing and question answering competition. *BMC Bioinformatics*, 16(1):138.

I. Tsochantaridis, T. Hofmann, T. Joachims, and Y. Altun. 2004. Support vector machine learning for interdependent and structured output spaces. In *ICML*, pages 104–114, Banff, Alberta, Canada,.

S. Varges, H. Bieler, M. Stede, L. C. Faulstich, K. Irsig, and M. Atalla. 2012. SemScribe: Natural language generation for medical reports. In *LREC*, pages 2674–2681, Istanbul, Turkey.

R. Vedantam, Z. C. L. Zitnick, and D. Parikh. 2015. CIDEr: Consensus-based image description evaluation. In *CVPR*, Boston, MA, USA.

O. Vinyals, A. Toshev, S. Bengio, and D. Erhan. 2015. Show and tell: A neural image caption generator. In *CVPR*, pages 3156–3164, Boston, MA, USA.

B. D. de Vos, J. M. Wolterink, P. A. de Jong, M. A. Viergever, and I. Išgum. 2016. 2D image classification for 3D anatomy localization: Employing deep convolutional neural networks. In *Medical Imaging: Image Processing*.

X. Wang, Y. Peng, L. Lu, Z. Lu, M. Bagheri, and R. M. Summers. 2017. ChestX-ray8: Hospital-scale chest X-ray database and benchmarks on weakly-supervised classification and localization of common thorax diseases. In *CVPR*, pages 2097–2106, Hawaii, HI, USA.

X. Wang, Y. Peng, L. Lu, Z. Lu, and R. M. Summers. 2018. TieNet: Text-image embedding network for common thorax disease classification and reporting in chest X-rays. In *CCPVR*, pages 9049–9058, Quebec City, Canada.

K. Xu, J. Ba, R. Kiros, K. Cho, A. Courville, R. Salakhudinov, R. Zemel, and Y. Bengio. 2015. Show, attend and tell: Neural image caption generation with visual attention. In *ICML*, pages 2048–2057, Lille, France.

X. Yang, R. Kwitt, and M. Niethammer. 2016. Fast predictive image registration. In *Deep Learning and Data Labeling for Medical Applications*, pages 48–57, Athens, Greece.

Q. You, H. Jin, Z. Wang, C. Fang, and J. Luo. 2016. Image captioning with semantic attention. In *CVPR*, pages 4651–4659, Las Vegas, NV, USA.

Y. Zhang, X. Wang, Z. Guo, and J. Li. 2018. ImageSem at ImageCLEF 2018 caption task: Image retrieval and transfer learning. In *CLEF CEUR Workshop*, Avignon, France.

Z. Zhang, P. Chen, M. Sapkota, and L. Yang. 2017a. TandemNet: Distilling knowledge from medical images using diagnostic reports as optional semantic references. In *International Conference on Medical Image Computing and Computer Assisted Intervention*, pages 320–328, Quebec City, Canada.

Z. Zhang, Y. Xie, F. Xing, M. McGough, and L. Yang. 2017b. MDNet: A semantically and visually interpretable medical image diagnosis network. In *CCPVR*, pages 6428–6436, Honolulu, HI, USA.

Revisiting Visual Grounding

Erik Conser
Computer Science Department
Portland State University
econser@pdx.edu

Kennedy Hahn
Computer Science Department
Portland State University
kehahn@pdx.edu

Chandler M. Watson
Computer Science Department
Stanford University
chandler.watson@stanford.edu

Melanie Mitchell
Computer Science Department
Portland State University
and Santa Fe Institute
mm@pdx.edu

Abstract

We revisit a particular visual grounding method: the "Image Retrieval Using Scene Graphs" (IRSG) system of Johnson et al. (2015). Our experiments indicate that the system does not effectively use its learned object-relationship models. We also look closely at the IRSG dataset, as well as the widely used Visual Relationship Dataset (VRD) that is adapted from it. We find that these datasets exhibit biases that allow methods that ignore relationships to perform relatively well. We also describe several other problems with the IRSG dataset, and report on experiments using a subset of the dataset in which the biases and other problems are removed. Our studies contribute to a more general effort: that of better understanding what machine learning methods that combine language and vision actually learn and what popular datasets actually test.

1 Introduction

Visual grounding is the general task of locating the components of a structured description in an image. In the visual-grounding literature, the structured description is often a natural-language phrase that has been parsed as a *scene graph* or as a *subject-predicate-object* triple. As one example of a visual-grounding challenge, Figure 1 illustrates the "Image Retrieval using Scene Graphs" (IRSG) task (Johnson et al., 2015). Here the sentence "A standing woman wearing dark sunglasses" is converted to a scene-graph representation (right) with nodes corresponding to objects, attributes, and relationships. Given a scene graph and an input image, the grounding task is to create bounding boxes corresponding to the specified objects, such that the located objects have the specified attributes and relationships (left). A final energy score reflects the quality of the match between the scene graph and the located boxes (lower is better), and can be used to rank images in a retrieval task. A second example of visual grounding, illustrated in Figure 2, is the "Referring Relationships" (RR) task of Krishna et al. (2018). Here, a sentence (e.g., "A horse following a person") is represented as a subject-predicate-object triple ("horse", "following", "person"). Given a triple and an input image, the task is to create bounding boxes corresponding to the named subject and object, such that the located boxes fit the specified predicate. Visual grounding tasks—at the intersection of vision and language—have become a popular area of research in machine learning, with the potential of improving automated image editing, captioning, retrieval, and question-answering, among other tasks.

While deep neural networks have produced impressive progress in object detection, visual-grounding tasks remain highly challenging. On the language side, accurately transforming a natural language phrase to a structured description can be difficult. On the vision side, the challenge is to learn—in a way that can be generalized—visual features of objects and attributes as well as flexible models of spatial and other relationships, and then to apply these models to figure out which of a given object class (e.g., *woman*) is the one referred to, sometimes locating small objects and recog-

Proceedings of the Second Workshop on Shortcomings in Vision and Language, pages 37–46
Minneapolis, USA, June 6, 2019. ©2017 Association for Computational Linguistics

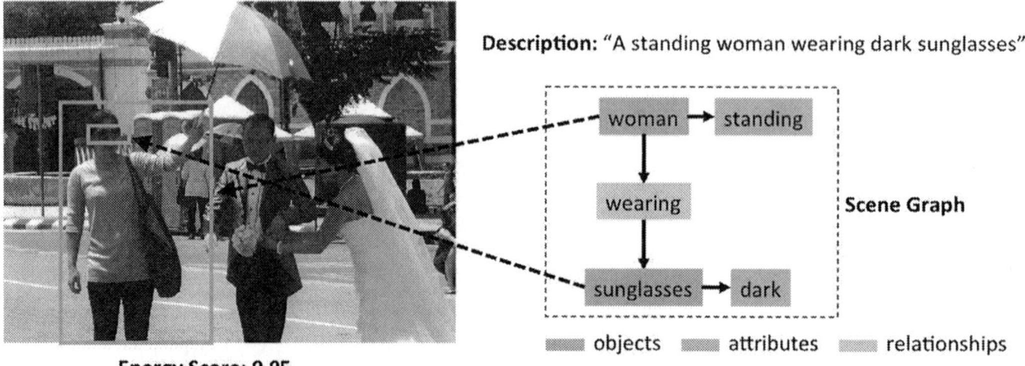

Figure 1: An example of the scene-graph-grounding task of Johnson et al. (2015). Right: A phrase represented as a scene graph. Left: A candidate grounding of the scene graph in a test image, here yielding a low energy score (lower is better).

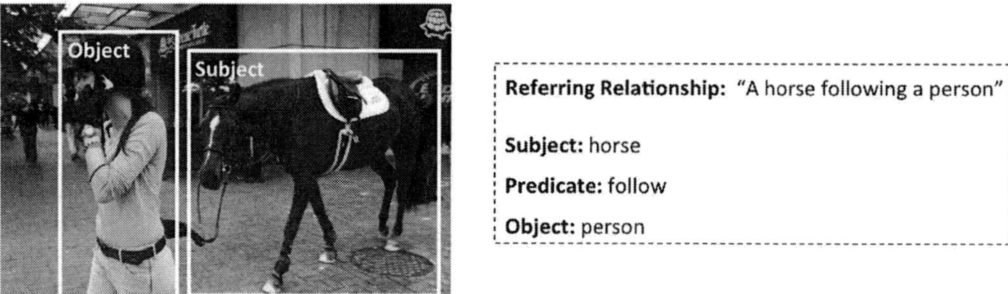

Figure 2: An example of the referring-relationship-grounding task of Krishna et al. (2018). Right: A phrase broken into subject, predicate, and object categories. Left: a candidate grounding of subject and object in a test image.

nizing hard-to-see attributes (e.g., *dark* vs. *clear* glasses). To date, the performance of machine learning systems on visual-grounding tasks with real-world datasets has been relatively low compared to human performance.

In addition, some in the machine-vision community have questioned the effectiveness of popular datasets that have been developed to evaluate the performance of systems on visual grounding tasks like the ones illustrated in Figures 1 and 2. Recently Cirik et al. (2018b) showed that for the widely used dataset Google-Ref (Mao et al., 2016), the task of grounding referring expressions has exploitable biases: for example, a system that predicts only object categories—ignoring relationships and attributes—still performs well on this task. Jabri et al. (2016) report related biases in visual question-answering datasets.

In this paper we re-examine the visual grounding approach of Johnson et al. (2015) to determine how well this system is actually performing scene-graph grounding. In particular, we compare this system with a simple baseline method to test if the original system is using information from object relationships, as claimed by Johnson et al. (2015). In addition, we investigate possible biases and other problems with the dataset used by Johnson et al. (2015), a version of which has also been used in many later studies. We briefly survey related work in visual grounding, and discuss possible future studies in this area.

2 Image Retrieval Using Scene Graphs

2.1 Methods

The "Image Retrieval Using Scene Graphs" (IRSG) method (Johnson et al., 2015) performs the task illustrated in Figure 1: given an input image and a scene graph, output a *grounding* of the scene graph in the image and an accompanying energy score. The grounding consists of a set of bounding boxes, each one corresponding to an object named in the scene graph, with the goal that the grounding gives the the best possible fit to the objects, attributes, and relationships specified in the scene graph. Note that the system described in (Johnson et al., 2015) does not perform any linguistic analysis; it assumes that a natural-language description has already been transformed into a scene graph.

The IRSG system is trained on a set of human-annotated images in which bounding boxes are labeled with object categories and attributes, and pairs of bounding boxes are labeled with relationships. The system learns appearance models for all object and attribute categories in the training set, and relationship models for all training-set relationships. The appearance model for object categories is learned as a convolutional neural network (CNN), which inputs an bounding box from an image and outputs a probability distribution over all object categories. The appearance model for object attributes is also learned as a CNN; it inputs an image bounding box and outputs a probability distribution over all attribute categories. The pairwise spatial relationship models are learned as Gaussian mixture models (GMMs); each GMM inputs a pair of bounding boxes from an image and outputs a probability density reflecting how well the GMM judges the input boxes to fit the model's corresponding spatial relationship (e.g., "woman wearing sunglasses"). Details of the training procedures are given in (Johnson et al., 2015).

After training is completed, the IRSG system can be run on test images. Given a test image and a scene graph, IRSG attempts to ground the scene graph in the image as follows. First the system creates a set of candidate bounding boxes using the Geodesic Object Proposal method (Krähenbühl and Koltun, 2014). The object and attribute CNNs are then used to assign probability distributions over all object and attribute categories to each candidate bounding box. Next, for each relationship in the scene graph, the GMM corresponding to that relationship assigns a probability density to each pair of candidate bounding boxes. The probability density is calibrated by Platt scaling (Platt, 2000) to provide a value representing the probability that the given pair of boxes is in the specified relationship.

Finally, these object and relationship probabilities are used to configure a conditional random field, implemented as factor graph. The objects and attributes are unary factors in the factor graph, each with one value for each image bounding box. The relationships are binary factors, with one value for each pair of bounding boxes. This factor graph represents the probability distribution of groundings conditioned on the scene graph and bounding boxes. Belief propagation (Andres et al., 2012) is then run on the factor graph to determine which candidate bounding boxes produce the lowest-energy grounding of the given scene graph. The output of the system is this grounding, along with its energy. The lower the energy, the better the predicted fit between the image and the scene graph.

To use the IRSG system in image retrieval, with a query represented as a scene graph, the IRSG system applies the grounding procedure for the given scene graph to every image in the test set, and ranks the resulting images in order of increasing energy. The highest ranking (lowest energy) images can be returned as the results of the query.

Johnson et al. (2015) trained and tested the IRSG method on an image dataset consisting of 5,000 images, split into 4,000 training images and 1,000 testing images. The objects, attributes, and relationships in each image were annotated by Amazon Mechanical Turk workers; the authors created scene graphs that captured the annotations. IRSG was tested on two types of scene-graph queries: full and partial. Each full scene-graph query was a highly detailed description of a single image in the test set—the average full scene graph consisted of 14 objects, 19 attributes, and 22 relationships. The partial scene graphs were generated by examination of subgraphs of the full scene graphs. Each combination of two objects, one relation, and one or two attributes was drawn from each full scene graph, and any partial scene graph that was found at least five times was added to the collection of partial queries. Johnson et al. randomly selected 119 partial queries to constitute the test set for partial queries.

2.2 Original Results

Johnson et al. (2015) used a "recall at k" metric to measure their their system's image retrieval performance. In experiments on both full and partial scene-graph queries, the authors found that their method outperformed several baselines. In particular, it outperformed—by a small degree—two "ablated" forms of their method: the first in which only object probabilities were used (attribute and relationship probabilities were ignored), and the second in which both object and attribute probabilities were used but relationship probabilities were ignored.

3   Revisiting IRSG

We obtained the IRSG code from the authors (Johnson et al., 2015), and attempted to replicate their reported results on the partial scene graphs. (Our study included only the partial scene graphs, which seemed to us to be a more realistic use case for image retrieval than the complex full graphs, each of which described only one image in the set.) We performed additional experiments in order to answer the following questions: (1) Does using relationship information in addition to object information actually help the system's performance? (2) Does the dataset used in this study have exploitable biases, similar to the findings of Cirik et al. (2018b) on the Google-Ref dataset? Note that here we use the term "bias" to mean any aspect of the dataset that allows a learning algorithm to rely on shallow correlations, rather than actually solving the intended task. (3) If the dataset does contain biases, how would IRSG perform on a dataset that did not contain such biases?

3.1   Comparing IRSG with an Object-Only Baseline

To investigate the first two questions, we created a baseline image-retrieval method that uses information only from object probabilities. Given a test image and a scene-graph query, we ran IRSG's Geodesic Object Proposal method on the test image to obtain bounding boxes, and we ran IRSG's trained CNN on each bounding box to obtain a probability for each object category. For each object category named in the query, our baseline method simply selects the bounding box with the highest probability for that query. No attribute or relationship information is used. We then use a *recall at k* ($R@k$) metric to compare the performance of our baseline method to that of the IRSG method.

Our $R@k$ metric was calculated as follows. For a given scene-graph query, let S_p be the set of *pos-*

itive images in the test set, where a positive image is one whose ground-truth object, attribute, and relationship labels match the query. Let S_n be the set of negative images in the test set. For each scene-graph query, IRSG was run on both S_p and S_n, returning an energy score for each image with respect to the scene graph. For each image we also computed a second score: the geometric mean of the highest object-category probabilities, as described above. The latter score ignored attribute and relationship information. We then rank-order each image in the test set by its score: for the IRSG method, scores (energy values—lower is better) are ranked in ascending order; for the baseline method, scores (geometric mean values—higher is better) are ranked in descending order. Because the size of S_p is different for different queries, we consider each positive image $I_p \in S_p$ separately. We put I_p alone in a pool with all the negative images, and ask if I_p is ranked in the top k. We define $R@k$ as the fraction of images in S_p that are top-k in this sense. For example, $R@1 = .2$ would mean that 20% of the positive images are ranked above all of the negative images for this query; $R@2 = .3$ would mean that 30% of the positive images are ranked above all but at most one of the negative images, and so on. This metric is slightly different from—and, we believe, provides a more useful evaluation than—the recall at k metric used in (Johnson et al., 2015), which only counted the position of the top-ranked positive image for each query in calculating $R@k$.

We computed $R@k$ in this way for each of the 150 partial scene graphs that were available in the test set provided by Johnson et al., and then averaged the 150 values at each k. The results are shown in Figure 3, for $k = 1, ..., 1000$. It can be seen that the two curves are nearly identical. Our result differs in a small degree from the results reported in (Johnson et al., 2015), in which IRSG performed slightly but noticeably better than an object-only version. The difference might be due to differences in the particular subset of scene-graph queries they used (they randomly selected 119, which were not listed in their paper), or to the slightly different $R@k$ metrics.

Our results imply that, contrary to expectations, IRSG performance does not benefit from the system's relationship models. (IRSG performance also does not seem to benefit from the system's attribute models, but here we focus on the role of

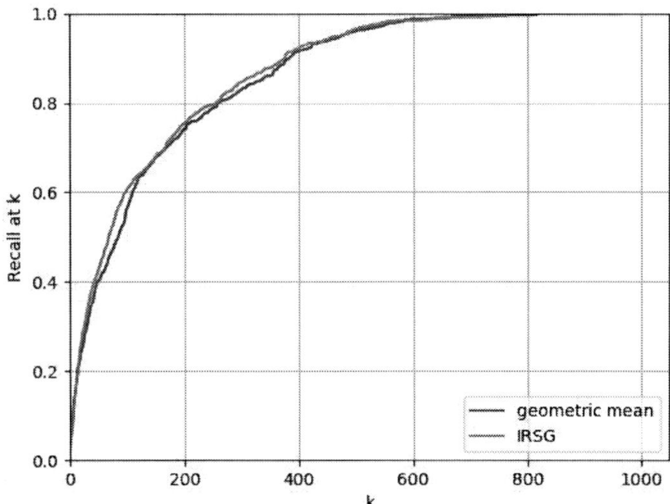

Figure 3: Recall at k values for IRSG and the geometric-mean baseline on the partial query dataset from (Johnson et al., 2015). This figure shows the averaged $R@k$ values for all partial scene-graph queries.

relationships.) There are two possible reasons for this: (1) the object-relationship models (Gaussian mixture models) in IRSG are not capturing useful information; or (2) there are biases in the dataset that allow successful scene-graph grounding without any information from object relationships. Our studies show that both hypotheses are correct.

Figure 4 shows results that support the first hypothesis. If, for a given scene-graph query, we look at IRSG's lowest-energy configuration of bounding boxes for every image, and compare the full (object-attribute-relationship) factorization (product of probabilities) to the factorization without relationships, we can see that the amount of information provided by the relationships is quite small. For example, for the query "clear glasses on woman", Figure 4 is a scatter plot in which each point represents an image in the test set. The x-axis values give the products of IRSG-assigned probabilities for objects and attributes in the scene graph, and the y-axis values give the full product—that is, including the relationship probabilities. If the relationship probabilities added useful information, we would expect a non-linear relationship between the x- and y-axis values. However, the plot generally shows a simple linear relationship (linear regression goodness-of-fit $r^2 = 0.97$), which indicates that the relationship distribution is not adding significant informa-

tion to the final grounding energy. We found that over 90% of the queries exhibited very strong linear relationships ($r^2 \geq 0.8$) of this kind. This suggests that the relationship probabilities computed by the GMMs are not capturing useful information.

We investigated the second hypothesis—that there are biases in the dataset that allow successful object grounding without relationship information—by a manual inspection of the 150 scene-graph queries and a sample of the 1,000 test images. We found two types of such biases. In the first type, a positive test image for a given query contains only one instance of each query object, which makes relationship information superfluous. For example, when given a query such as "standing man wearing shirt" there is no need to distinguish which is the particular "standing man" who is wearing a "shirt": there is only one of each. In the second type of bias, a positive image for a given query contains multiple instances of the query objects, but *any* of the instances would be a correct grounding for the query. For example, when given the query "black tire on road", even if there are many different tires in the image, all of them are black and all of them are on the road. Thus any black-tire grounding will be correct. Time constraints prevented us from making a precise count of instances of these biases for each

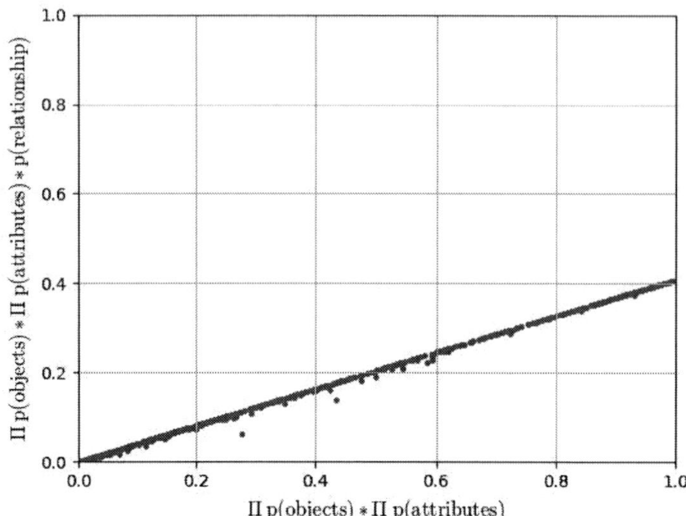

Figure 4: A scatterplot of the factorizations for a single query in the original dataset ("clear glasses on woman"), each point representing a single image. The x-axis value is the product of the object and attribute probability values from IRSG's lowest-energy grounding on this image. The y-axis value includes the product of the relationship probabilities. A strong relationship model would modify the object-attribute factorization and create a larger spread of values than what is evident in this figure. We found similar strongly linear relationships for over 90% of the queries in the test set.

query, but our sampling suggested that examples of such biases occur in the positive test images for at least half of the queries.

A closer look at the dataset and queries revealed several additional issues that make it difficult to evaluate the performance of a visual grounding system. While Johnson et al. (2015) reported averages over many partial scene-graph queries, these averages were biased by the fact that in several cases essentially same query appeared more than once in the set, sometimes using synonymous terms (e.g., "bus on gray street" and "bus on gray road" are counted as separate queries, as are "man on bench" and "sitting man on bench"). Removing duplicates of this kind decreases the original set of 150 queries to 105 unique queries. Going further, we found that some queries included two instances of a single object class: for example, "standing man next to man". We found that when given such queries, the IRSG system would typically create two bounding boxes around the same object in the image (e.g., the "standing man" and the other man would be grounded as the same person).

Additionally, there are typically very few positive images per query in the test set. The mean number of positive images per query is 6.5, and the median number is 5. The dataset would benefit from a greater number of positive results for more thorough testing results.

The dataset was annotated by Amazon Mechanical Turk workers using an open annotation scheme, rather than directing the workers to select from a specific set of classes, attributes, and relationships. Due to the open scheme, there are numerous errors that affect a system's learning potential, including mislabeled objects and relationships, as well as typographical errors (refridgerator [*sic*]), synonyms (kid/child, man/guy/boy/person), and many prominent objects left unlabeled. These errors can lead to false negatives during testing.

3.2 Testing IRSG on "Clean" Queries and Data

To assess the performance of IRSG without the complications of many of these data and query issues, we created seven queries—involving only objects and relationships, no attributes—that avoided many of the ambiguities described above. We made sure that there were at least 10 positive test-set examples for each query, and we fixed the labeling in the training and test data to make sure that all objects named in these queries were correctly labeled. The queries (and number of positive examples for each in the test set) are the following:

- Person Has Beard: 96

- Person Wearing Helmet: 81

- Person Wearing Sunglasses: 79

- Pillow On Couch: 38

- Person On Skateboard: 29

- Person On Bench: 18

- Person On Horse: 13

We call this set of queries, along with their training and test examples, the "clean dataset".

Using only these queries, we repeated the comparison between IRSG and the geometric-mean baseline described above. The $R@k$ results are shown in Figure 5. These results are very similar to those in Figure 3. This result indicates that, while the original dataset exhibits biases and other problems that make the original system hard to evaluate, it still seems that relationship probabilities do not provide strongly distinguishing information to the other components of the IRSG method. The lack of strong relationship performance was also seen in (Quinn et al., 2018) where the IRSG and object-only baseline method showed almost identical $R@k$ performance on a different, larger dataset.

4 Revisiting "Referring Relationship" Grounding

The IRSG task is closely related to the "Referring Relationships" (RR) task, proposed by Krishna et al. (2018) and illustrated in Figure 2. The method developed by Krishna et al. uses iterative attention to shift between image regions according to the given predicate, in order to locate subject and object. The authors evaluated their model on several datasets, including the same images as were in the IRSG dataset (here called "VRD" or "visual relationship dataset"), but with 4710 referring-relationship queries (several per test image). The evaluation metric they reported was mean *intersection over union* (IOU) of the subject and object detections with ground-truth boxes. This metric does not give information about the

detection rate. To investigate whether biases appear in this dataset and queries similar to the ones we described above, we again created a baseline method that used only object information. In particular, we used the VRD training set to fine-tune a pre-trained version[1] of the faster-RCNN object-detection method (Ren et al., 2015) on the object categories that appear in the VRD dataset. We then ran faster-RCNN on each test image, and for each query selected the highest-confidence bounding box for the subject and object categories. (If the query subject and object were the same category, we randomly assigned subject and object to the highest and second-highest confidence boxes.) Finally, for each query, we manually examined visualizations of the predicted subject and object boxes in each test image to determine whether the subject and object boxes fit the subject, object, and predicate of the query. We found that for 56% of the image/query pairs, faster-RCNN had identified correct subject and object boxes. In short, our object-only baseline was able to correctly locate the subject and object 56% of the time, using no relationship information. This indicates significant biases in the dataset, which calls into question any published referring-relationship results on this dataset that does not compare with this baseline. In future work we plan to replicate the results reported by Krishna et al. (2018) and to compare it with our object-only baseline. We hope to do the same for other published results on referring relationships using the VRD dataset, among other datasets (Cirik et al., 2018a; Liu et al., 2019; Raboh et al., 2019).

5 Related Work

Other groups have explored grounding single objects referred to by natural-language expressions (Hu et al., 2016; Nagaraja et al., 2016; Hu et al., 2017; Zhang et al., 2018) and grounding all nouns mentioned in a natural language phrase (Rohrbach et al., 2016; Plummer et al., 2017, 2018; Yeh et al., 2017).

Visual grounding is different from, though related to, tasks such as visual relationship detection (Lu et al., 2016), in which the task is not to ground a particular phrase in an image, but to detect *all* known relationships. The VRD dataset we

---

[1] We used `faster_rcnn_resnet101_coco` from `https://github.com/tensorflow/models/blob/master/research/object_detection/g3doc/detection_model_zoo.md`.

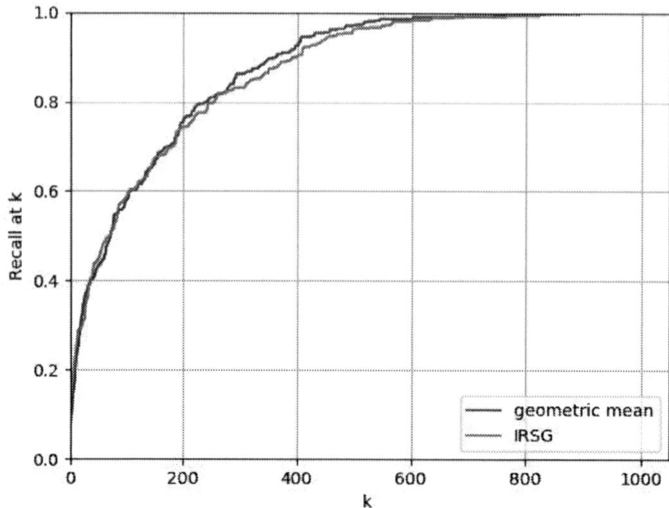

Figure 5: $R@k$ values for the IRSG model and geometric mean model on the clean dataset. This figure shows, for each k, the averaged $R@k$ values over the seven queries.

described above is commonly used in visual relationship detection tasks, and to our knowledge there are no prior studies of bias and other problems in this dataset.

It should be noted that visual grounding also differs from automated caption generation (Xu et al., 2015) and automated scene graph generation (Xu et al., 2017), which input an image and output a natural language phrase or a scene graph, respectively.

The diversity of datasets used in these various studies as well as the known biases and other problems in many widely used datasets makes it difficult to determine the state of the art in visual grounding tasks as well as related tasks such as visual relationship detection.

6   Conclusions and Future Work

We have closely investigated one highly cited approach to visual grounding, the IRSG method of (Johnson et al., 2015). We demonstrated that this method does not perform better than a simple object-only baseline, and does not seem to use information from relationships between objects, contrary to the authors' claims, at least on the original dataset of partial scene graphs as well as on our "clean" version. We have also identified exploitable biases and other problems associated with this dataset, as well as with the version used

in Krishna et al. (2018).

Our work can be seen as a contribution to the effort promoted by Cirik et al. (2018b): "to make meaningful progress on grounded language tasks, we need to pay careful attention to what and how our models are learning, and whether or datasets contain exploitable bias." In future work, we plan to investigate other prominent algorithms and datasets for visual grounding, as well as to curate benchmarks without the biases and problems we described above. Some researchers have used synthetically generated data, such as the CLEVR set (Johnson et al., 2017); however to date the high performances of visual grounding systems on this dataset have not translated to high performance on real-world datasets (e.g., Krishna et al. (2018)). We also plan to explore alternative approaches to visual grounding tasks, such as the "active" approach described by Quinn et al. (2018).

Acknowledgments

We are grateful to Justin Johnson of Stanford University for sharing the source code for the IRSG project, and to NVIDIA corporation for donation of a GPU used for this work. We also thank the anonymous reviewers of this paper for several helpful suggestions for improvement. This material is based upon work supported by the National Science Foundation under Grant Number

IIS-1423651. Any opinions, findings, and conclusions or recommendations expressed in this material are those of the authors and do not necessarily reflect the views of the National Science Foundation.

References

Bjoern Andres, Thorsten Beier, and Jörg H. Kappes. 2012. OpenGM: A C++ library for discrete graphical models. *arXiv preprint arXiv:1206.0111*.

Volkan Cirik, Taylor Berg-Kirkpatrick, and Louis-Philippe Morency. 2018a. Using syntax to ground referring expressions in natural images. In *Proceedings of the Thirty-Second Conference on Artificial Intelligence (AAAI)*, pages 6756–6764. AAAI.

Volkan Cirik, Louis-Philippe Morency, and Taylor Berg-Kirkpatrick. 2018b. Visual referring expression recognition: What do systems actually learn? In *Proceedings of NAACL-HLT 2018*, pages 781–787.

Ronghang Hu, Marcus Rohrbach, Jacob Andreas, Trevor Darrell, and Kate Saenko. 2017. Modeling relationships in referential expressions with compositional modular networks. In *Proceedings of the IEEE Conference on Computer Vision and Pattern Recognition (CVPR)*, pages 1115–1124.

Ronghang Hu, Huazhe Xu, Marcus Rohrbach, Jiashi Feng, Kate Saenko, and Trevor Darrell. 2016. Natural language object retrieval. In *Proceedings of the IEEE Conference on Computer Vision and Pattern Recognition*, pages 4555–4564.

Allan Jabri, Armand Joulin, and Laurens Van Der Maaten. 2016. Revisiting visual question answering baselines. In *European Conference on Computer Vision (ECCV)*, pages 727–739. Springer.

Justin Johnson, Bharath Hariharan, Laurens van der Maaten, Li Fei-Fei, C Lawrence Zitnick, and Ross Girshick. 2017. CLEVR: A diagnostic dataset for compositional language and elementary visual reasoning. In *Proceedings of the IEEE Conference on Computer Vision and Pattern Recognition (CVPR)*, pages 2901–2910.

Justin Johnson, Ranjay Krishna, Michael Stark, Li-Jia Li, David Shamma, Michael Bernstein, and Li Fei-Fei. 2015. Image retrieval using scene graphs. In *Proceedings of the IEEE Conference on Computer Vision and Pattern Recognition (CVPR)*, pages 3668–3678.

Philipp Krähenbühl and Vladlen Koltun. 2014. Geodesic object proposals. In *Proceedings of the European Conference on Computer Vision (ECCV)*, pages 725–739.

Ranjay Krishna, Ines Chami, Michael Bernstein, and Li Fei-Fei. 2018. Referring relationships. In *Proceedings of the IEEE Conference on Computer Vision and Pattern Recognition (CVPR)*, pages 6867–6876.

Xihui Liu, Wang Zihao, Jing Shao, Xiaogang Wang, and Hongsheng Li. 2019. Improving referring expression grounding with cross-modal attention-guided erasing. *arXiv preprint arXiv:1903.00839*.

Cewu Lu, Ranjay Krishna, Michael Bernstein, and Li Fei-Fei. 2016. Visual relationship detection with language priors. In *European Conference on Computer Vision (ECCV)*, pages 852–869. Springer.

Junhua Mao, Jonathan Huang, Alexander Toshev, Oana Camburu, Alan L. Yuille, and Kevin Murphy. 2016. Generation and comprehension of unambiguous object descriptions. In *Proceedings of the IEEE Conference on Computer Vision and Pattern Recognition (CVPR)*, pages 11–20.

Varun K. Nagaraja, Vlad I. Morariu, and Larry S. Davis. 2016. Modeling context between objects for referring expression understanding. In *European Conference on Computer Vision (ECCV)*, pages 792–807. Springer.

John C. Platt. 2000. Probabilistic outputs for support vector machines and comparisons to regularized likelihood methods. In *Advances in Large Margin Classifiers*. MIT Press.

Bryan A. Plummer, Arun Mallya, Christopher M. Cervantes, Julia Hockenmaier, and Svetlana Lazebnik. 2017. Phrase localization and visual relationship detection with comprehensive image-language cues. In *Proceedings of the IEEE International Conference on Computer Vision*, pages 1928–1937.

Bryan A. Plummer, Kevin J. Shih, Yichen Li, Ke Xu, Svetlana Lazebnik, Stan Sclaroff, and Kate Saenko. 2018. Open-vocabulary phrase detection. *arXiv preprint arXiv:1811.07212*.

Max H. Quinn, Erik Conser, Jordan M. Witte, and Melanie Mitchell. 2018. Semantic image retrieval via active grounding of visual situations. In *International Conference on Semantic Computing (ICSC)*, pages 172–179. IEEE.

Moshiko Raboh, Roei Herzig, Gal Chechik, Jonathan Berant, and Amir Globerson. 2019. Learning latent scene-graph representations for referring relationships. *arXiv preprint arXiv:1902.10200*.

Shaoqing Ren, Kaiming He, Ross Girshick, and Jian Sun. 2015. Faster R-CNN: Towards real-time object detection with region proposal networks. In *Advances in Neural Information Processing Systems*, pages 91–99.

Anna Rohrbach, Marcus Rohrbach, Ronghang Hu, Trevor Darrell, and Bernt Schiele. 2016. Grounding of textual phrases in images by reconstruction. In

European Conference on Computer Vision (ECCV), pages 817–834. Springer.

Danfei Xu, Yuke Zhu, Christopher B. Choy, and Li Fei-Fei. 2017. Scene graph generation by iterative message passing. In *Proceedings of the IEEE Conference on Computer Vision and Pattern Recognition*, pages 5410–5419.

Kelvin Xu, Jimmy Ba, Ryan Kiros, Kyunghyun Cho, Aaron Courville, Ruslan Salakhudinov, Rich Zemel, and Yoshua Bengio. 2015. Show, attend and tell: Neural image caption generation with visual attention. In *International conference on machine learning*, pages 2048–2057.

Raymond Yeh, Jinjun Xiong, Wen-Mei Hwu, Minh Do, and Alexander Schwing. 2017. Interpretable and globally optimal prediction for textual grounding using image concepts. In *Advances in Neural Information Processing Systems*, pages 1912–1922.

Hanwang Zhang, Yulei Niu, and Shih-Fu Chang. 2018. Grounding referring expressions in images by variational context. In *Proceedings of the IEEE Conference on Computer Vision and Pattern Recognition*, pages 4158–4166.

The Steep Road to Happily Ever After: An Analysis of Current Visual Storytelling Models

Yatri Modi and **Natalie Parde**
Department of Computer Science
University of Illinois at Chicago
{ymodi2, parde}@uic.edu

Abstract

Visual storytelling is an intriguing and complex task that only recently entered the research arena. In this work, we survey relevant work to date, and conduct a thorough error analysis of three very recent approaches to visual storytelling. We categorize and provide examples of common types of errors, and identify key shortcomings in current work. Finally, we make recommendations for addressing these limitations in the future.

1 Introduction

Artificial intelligence continues to evolve, making it increasingly plausible to develop models that interpret vision and language in a humanlike manner. A crucial element of such models is the capacity to not only match images with surface-level descriptions, but to infer deeper contextual meaning. Recent literature has begun to refer to this task as *visual storytelling*: the generation of a cohesive, sequential set of natural-language descriptions across multiple images (Huang et al., 2016). Visual storytelling is distinct from image captioning in that the text generated is oftentimes subjective, hinges on contextual image order, and typically employs more abstract and dynamic terms. We illustrate the dichotomy between the two more concretely in terms of possible sets of sentences[1] for the images in Figure 1.

Sentence Set 1: (1) *A woman looking at a collection of tribal masks on the wall.* (2) *Three skulls of varying sizes ordered from largest to smallest.* (3) *A top view of a book about mythical creatures.* (4) *Three people standing in a store looking at the products.* (5) *An old traveling wagon that is on display.*

---

[1] Real samples (with punctuation and capitalization edited in some cases to increase readability) from the VIST dataset: `http://visionandlanguage.net/VIST/dataset.html`

Figure 1: A sequence of images from the VIST dataset.

Sentence Set 2: (1) *I went to the natural history museum today.* (2) *Their evolution display was very interesting.* (3) *They had an area for cryptozoology.* (4) *They also have a gift shop.* (5) *My favorite was this real covered wagon from 200 years ago.*

The first is a set of traditional image captions, whereas the latter represents a visual story. Note that the former presents factual descriptions of the images in isolation from one another. The latter also describes the images, but places stronger emphasis on the development of a cohesive narrative underlying the image sequence.

High-performing visual storytelling approaches will enable growth for a variety of applications, many of which are associated with language understanding tasks. They may also hold promise as a tool for assistive technology. For instance, it is relatively common for users to upload large photo albums to social media platforms without including any image descriptions at all, making these albums inaccessible to those with sight impairments. Visual storytelling could bridge this gap by automatically generating descriptive narratives for these albums.

Despite recent interest in visual storytelling, fu-

Proceedings of the Second Workshop on Shortcomings in Vision and Language, pages 47–57
Minneapolis, USA, June 6, 2019. ©2017 Association for Computational Linguistics

eled by the 2018 Visual Storytelling Challenge,[2] this research area is still quite nascent. To date, no comprehensive review has been made of work on the task. Such an analysis is necessary to spur additional research and recommend directions for future work. Here, we fill this void, making the following contributions:

- We catalogue existing models for visual storytelling, comparing and contrasting them with one another.

- We provide a performance comparison based on the original results (when publicly available) or re-implementations (when not).

- We categorize errors into distinct types and compile statistics indicating their frequencies within and across models.

- We make recommendations for addressing these errors in future visual storytelling models.

We discuss relevant prior work in Section 2, and describe the dataset used for visual storytelling tasks in Section 3. In Section 4 we present an overview of the models included in our analysis, and in Section 5 we explain how these models were evaluated. We conduct our comprehensive error analysis in Section 6, and make our recommendations based on the outcomes of this analysis in Section 7. We summarize these sections and report our final conclusions in Section 8.

2 Related Work

We focus our analysis on methods employed by teams that participated in the 2018 Visual Storytelling Challenge. The challenge required participants to make AI systems capable of generating human-like stories from a sequence of images as input. It had (1) an *Internal Track* that constrained participants such that they could train only on data from the Visual Storytelling (VIST) Dataset, described further in Section 3, and use pretraining data only from any version of the ImageNet Large Scale Visual Recognition Challenge (ILSVRC)[3]

and any version of the Penn Treebank;[4] and (2) an *External Track* that allowed participants free reign when training, with the only requirement being that all training data be made publicly accessible if it was not already. The challenge evaluated the quality of the generated stories using both an automatic metric (METEOR (Banerjee and Lavie, 2005), described in further detail in Section 5.2) and human ratings corresponding to the following characteristics: (1) focus, (2) structure and coherence, (3) inclination to share, (4) likelihood of being written by a human, (5) visual grounding quality, and (6) level of detail.[5] The winning team for the challenge was DG-DLMX (Gonzalez-Rico and Pineda, 2018).

We perform an in-depth error analysis of the work done by UCSB-NLP (Wang et al., 2018), SnuBiVtt (Kim et al., 2018), and DG-DLMX (Gonzalez-Rico and Pineda, 2018) for the Visual Storytelling Challenge; these are the three teams who have released publicly available source code to date. We describe their models in further detail in Sections 4.1-4.3. The other team participating in the challenge was NLPSA501 (Hsu et al., 2018). NLPSA501 introduced a convolutional neural network (CNN) and gated recurrent unit (GRU) encoder-decoder model that incorporated an inter-sentence diverse beam search as a way to reduce redundancy in the generated stories. We could not analyze their model's output as we did for those by UCSB-NLP, DG-DLMX and Snu-BiVtt, due to the lack of available implementations or generated stories.

Outside of the Visual Storytelling Challenge, several other groups have explored the task of visual storytelling. Huang et al. (2016) published the original paper introducing the visual storytelling task, comparing storytelling with image captioning. The authors used GRUs for both encoding the image and decoding the story. Lukin et al. (2018) defined a pipeline for visual storytelling consisting of Object Detection, Single-Image Inferencing, and Multi-Image Narration steps. Yu et al. (2017) employed an alternate pipeline comprised of Album Encoder, Photo Selector, and Story Generator stages. Agrawal et al.'s (2016) approach focuses on identifying

---

[2]https://evalai.cloudcv.org/web/challenges/challenge-page/76/overview

[3]A well-known annual competition that challenges researchers to solve a variety of large-scale object and image detection tasks (Russakovsky et al., 2015): http://image-net.org/challenges/LSVRC/.

[4]A highly popular English-language part-of-speech tagset (Marcus et al., 1993): https://catalog.ldc.upenn.edu/LDC99T42.

[5]Human judgements were solicited using Amazon Mechanical Turk (https://www.mturk.com/).

proper sequences for existing story sentences, rather than on generating those sentences themselves. Finally, Jain et al. (2017) explored a phrase-based and syntax-based statistical machine translation approach as a vehicle for story generation using text but no images from the VIST dataset. The approaches developed for the Visual Storytelling Challenge were designed to be improvements upon Huang et al.'s (2016) model. Although the approaches explored outside the challenge are not publicly available, we consider them when making our general recommendations.

The task of visual storytelling is still in its infancy, and to date there exists no comprehensive review of prior work in this area. Our analysis fills this void, by summarizing relevant work in a shared context and providing concrete comparisons and example output when possible. This allows us to identify core areas for improvement in future implementations, and recommend specific actions to address these current limitations. Our hope is that this analysis can serve as a useful launchpad for other researchers aspiring to work in the visual storytelling domain.

3 Data

Most visual storytelling work to date has been trained and evaluated using the VIST Dataset (Huang et al., 2016). VIST is the first publicly available dataset for sequential vision-to-language tasks, and consists of sequences or "albums" of images wherein each image is paired with two types of captions; namely, descriptions of images in isolation (DII), and stories of images in sequence (SIS). The images were originally downloaded from Flickr (https://www.flickr.com/). In total, the dataset comprises 10,117 Flickr albums containing 210,819 unique photos.

Amazon Mechanical Turk (AMT) workers selected subsets of five images per album about which to write sequential, cohesive stories. The dataset contains 50,200 story sequences overall; these are divided into subsets of 40,155 training, 4,990 validation and 5,055 testing stories. Five written stories were collected per album. Three standalone descriptions per image (DII, first defined above) were also collected separately using the image captioning interface used to build the COCO image caption dataset (Lin et al., 2014). In both the stories and descriptions, all people names were replaced with generic MALE/FEMALE tokens, and all named entities were replaced with their entity type (e.g., location). A small number of broken images were filtered from VIST by most research groups. For concrete examples of DII and SIS from VIST, we refer readers to Figure 1, where Sentence Sets 1 and 2 (see Section 1) are from the DII and SIS subsets, respectively.

4 Methods

We analyze three of the approaches submitted to the Visual Storytelling Challenge: AREL (Wang et al., 2018), GLACNet (Kim et al., 2018) and Contextualize, Show and Tell (Gonzalez-Rico and Pineda, 2018). We selected these approaches as the focus of our work for two reasons. First, all were publicly available and well-documented, ensuring easy replicability. Other existing visual storytelling models (Huang et al., 2016; Agrawal et al., 2016; Yu et al., 2017; Hsu et al., 2018; Lukin et al., 2018) would have required reimplementation. Doing so introduces the possibility of unintentionally crippling performance (e.g., when setting required but unreported parameters), which we wished to avoid. Second, all were very recent models, representing the current state of the art in visual storytelling. We summarize AREL, GLACNet, and Contextualize, Show and Tell in Sections 4.1, 4.2, and 4.3, and refer readers to the original papers for fuller detail.

4.1 Adversarial Reward Learning (AREL)

AREL (Wang et al., 2018) is an adversarial reinforcement learning approach that makes use of two models: a policy model, followed by a reward model. The policy model is an encoder-decoder model utilizing a CNN-recurrent neural network (RNN) architecture, used to generate new stories. Specifically, a pre-trained CNN is fed a sequence of 5 images as input to extract high-level image features. These features are passed forward and further encoded as visual context vectors using bidirectional GRUs. The outputs of the encoder are then fed into a GRU-RNN decoder to generate sub-stories for the image sequence in parallel. The sub-stories are concatenated to form a single full story. The CNN-based reward model is applied to every sub-story to compute its partial reward, and from the input sequence embeddings, n-gram features are extracted using convolution kernels of different sizes and passed through pooling layers. Image features are concatenated with these sentence representations and passed through a fully connected layer to obtain the final reward. To perform adversarial reward learning, the models were alternately optimized using stochastic gradient descent. The objective of the story generation policy was to maximize the similarity between a Reward Boltzmann distribution and itself. The first model optimized the policy to minimize the KL divergence (Kullback and Leibler, 1951) between itself and the Boltzmann Distribution, and the second model attempted to (a) minimize the KL divergence with the empirical distribution, and (b) maximize the KL divergence with the approximated policy distribution, with the objective of distinguishing between human and machine generated stories.

Wang et al. (2018) demonstrated that AREL outperforms a generative adversarial network (GAN) model, a cross-entropy model, and other baselines and achieves state-of-the-art results across both automated and human metrics. The human metrics considered included both a Turing test (in which annotators attempted to guess which of two stories was written by a human) and pairwise comparisons measuring relevance, expressiveness, and concreteness.

4.2 GLocal Attention Cascading Networks (GLACNet)

GLACNet (Kim et al., 2018) also uses an encoder-decoder architecture, but it adds a hard attention mechanism which stresses feeding both the local image features and the overall context to the decoder as input. The image-specific features are extracted using a 152-layer residual network (He et al., 2016). Those features are fed sequentially into a bidirectional LSTM, which then produces the global context vectors. The global context and local image features are combined to form *glocal* vectors and passed through fully connected layers. The output is concatenated with word tokens and fed to the decoder (LSTM) as input. Thus, five glocal vectors for each image are fed into the decoder one after another, creating a cascading mechanism by passing the hidden state of one sentence generator as the initial hidden state of the next sentence generator.

To validate that all components of the GLACNet architecture contributed to the model's performance, Kim et al. (2018) conducted an ablation study in which the cascading, global attention, local attention, and post-processing routines were removed one at a time, comparing perplexity and METEOR (Banerjee and Lavie, 2005) scores between conditions as well as with a standalone LSTM sequence-to-sequence (Seq2Seq) model and the full GLACNet model. The full GLACNet model exhibited the best performance, and the other GLACNet-based models exhibited better performance than the LSTM Seq2Seq model, thereby verifying the utility of this approach.

4.3 Contextualize, Show and Tell

Contextualize, Show and Tell (Gonzalez-Rico and Pineda, 2018) won the 2018 Visual Storytelling Challenge. The model uses an encoder LSTM to read in the image representations one by one for every image in a sequence. The image representations are generated using Inception V3 (Szegedy et al., 2016). Five decoders, again LSTMs, then read in the image embedding as input. The first hidden state of each decoder is initialized using the last hidden state of the encoder to provide the model with global context. Gonzalez-Rico and Pineda (2018) obtained the final story by concatenating the outputs of the model's five decoders.

As part of the Visual Storytelling Challenge, the model was evaluated on public and hidden test sets using both human evaluation and an automated metric (METEOR). METEOR scores of 30.88 and 31 were obtained on the public and hidden test sets, respectively.[6] Human evaluation scores were collected via Amazon Mechanical Turk. Crowd workers evaluated six aspects of each story using a Likert scale. Each worker was asked to indicate the degree to which: 1) the story was focused, 2) the story had good structure and coherence, 3) the worker would share the story, 4) the worker thought the story was written by a human, 5) the story was visually grounded, and 6) the story was detailed. In summing the average scores received for each criterion, Gonzalez-Rico and Pineda's (2018) model achieved a score of 18.498, whereas human-generated stories achieved a score of 23.596.

5 Evaluation

5.1 Experimental Setup

We trained and evaluated AREL according to the instructions provided in its publicly available

---

[6]Gonzalez-Rico and Pineda (2018) reported a METEOR score of 34.4 on the standard VIST test set.

Model	METEOR	CIDEr	ROUGE-L	BLEU-1	BLEU-2	BLEU-3	BLEU-4	Perplexity
AREL-s-50	**34.9**	**9.1**	29.4	**62.9**	**38.4**	**22.7**	**14.0**	-
BLEU-RL	34.6	8.9	29.0	62.1	38.0	22.6	13.9	-
CIDEr-RL	**34.9**	8.1	**29.7**	61.9	37.8	22.5	13.8	-
GLACNet	30.14	-	-	-	-	-	-	**18.28**
Contextualize, Show and Tell	34.4	5.1	29.2	60.1	36.5	21.1	12.7	-

Table 1: Performance as reported in the source papers (Wang et al., 2018; Kim et al., 2018). BLEU-RL, METEOR-RL, and CIDEr-RL were baseline reinforcement learning approaches using BLEU, METEOR, and CIDEr scores as their reward functions, respectively (Wang et al., 2018).

Model	METEOR	CIDEr	ROUGE-L	BLEU-1	BLEU-2	BLEU-3	BLEU-4	Perplexity
AREL-s-50	**35.2**	**8.4**	**29.9**	61.9	**38.3**	**22.8**	**13.9**	-
GLACNet	29.46	3.7	28.2	53.4	29.4	15.6	8.6	**19.51**

Table 2: Performance obtained when we ran AREL-s-50 and GLACNet, the two models for which we were able to obtain working implementations.

Github repository.[7] However, we modified the source code slightly such that we were able to obtain the individual METEOR scores for each predicted story in the test set. This helped us in performing an in-depth error analysis of the generated stories and determining how well the automatic metrics were at scoring the stories. Training the model took around 2 weeks on a 3.5 GHz Intel Core i5 CPU with 16 GB RAM.[8]

The GLACNet code is also publicly available.[9] We trained and evaluated the model using an NVIDIA Tesla P100 GPU instance on Google Cloud Platform. The model took one week to finish training. The original source code only provided an average METEOR score across all generated stories after testing. Thus, we added code to produce the METEOR score for each story. We will make all adapted source code publicly available online to ensure easy replicability.

The source code for Contextualize, Show and Tell is available online as well.[10] The authors personally sent us the generated stories, so we did not re-implement their model. We have directly included their METEOR results in our evaluation.

5.2 Evaluation Metrics

Common metrics for evaluating visual storytelling models include METEOR (Banerjee and Lavie, 2005), BLEU (Papineni et al., 2002), CIDEr (Vedantam et al., 2015), and ROUGE-L (Lin and Och, 2004). METEOR, the primary metric considered in the Visual Storytelling Challenge, calculates the alignment between the machine-generated hypotheses and the reference stories based on the exact, stem, synonym, and paraphrase matches between words and phrases. While AREL was evaluated using METEOR as well as the other metrics, GLACNet was evaluated using only METEOR scores and measures of perplexity. Contextualize, Show and Tell was also evaluated using only METEOR. We generated scores for the remaining metrics as well for GLACNet and Contextualize, Show and Tell to aid our analysis.

5.3 Results

We observed slightly different results from those originally reported for the models included in our evaluation. We include both the originally-reported results and results based directly on original output files if available (Table 1) and our results from when we ran AREL and GLACNet (Table 2) in Tables 1 and 2. When we ran AREL and GLACNet, we collected scores for METEOR, CIDEr, ROUGE-L, BLEU-1, BLEU-2, BLEU-3, and BLEU-4, and found that AREL outperformed GLACNet in all cases (Table 2). We also found that based on Wang et al.'s (2018) and Gonzalez-Rico and Pineda's (2018) reported results and the additional metrics we computed for Contextualize, Show and Tell, the former outperformed the latter.

---

[7]https://github.com/littlekobe/AREL

[8]Extenuating circumstances limited our hardware resources in the midst of our AREL evaluation. Training would have undoubtedly been quicker using GPUs, as was done in the original paper (Wang et al., 2018).

[9]https://github.com/tkim-snu/GLACNet

[10]https://github.com/dgonzalez-ri/neural-visual-storyteller

6   Error Analysis

We defined a threshold METEOR score of 25, with stories scoring below this threshold considered as serious errors. This threshold was chosen following a manual assessment of the predicted stories, with METEOR < 25 representing a medium at which there existed both a sizable number of errors, and a sample of generated stories that were of noticeably low quality. Stories having a METEOR score $\geq$50 were also analyzed for any anomalies (e.g., bad stories with high scores).

Some metrics (CIDEr and BLEU-4) produced scores of 0 for many stories in both models. Upon manual analysis we found many of these stories to be sensible. Other work has confirmed that BLEU-3 and CIDEr scores do not correlate well with human evaluations (Wang et al., 2018).

We systematically analyzed each story in error and made notes indicating characteristics contributing to the error (including those that rendered the predicted stories to be completely meaningless or incoherent). In the process, we also identified mechanisms by which those errors may be addressed in the future. We compiled the errors into representative categories, which we define in Section 6.1 and exemplify in Table 3. We discuss these errors in fuller detail in Section 6.2. In Section 6.2 we also discuss some general errors from papers about other visual storytelling approaches for which we were unable to obtain full working implementations.

6.1   Error Categories

We define our representative error categories as follows:

- **Grammatical Errors:** Incorrect use of verbs and tenses and/or subject-verb disagreements.

- **Contradictions:** Presence of inconsistent ideas within the same story (e.g., two sub-stories that are the opposite of each other).

- **Repetitions:** These errors were further subdivided into the following categories.

    - **Repetitions within Story:** Recurrence of the same sentence(s) within a story.

    - **Repetitions within Sentence:** Recurrence of the same phrase(s) within a sub-story.

    - **Repetitive Subject:** The sub-stories have the same subject and differ only in the adjective used to describe it.

    - **Repetitive Sentence Structure:** Most sentences start with "the [noun] was/were/is [adjective]." This leads to monotonous and unoriginal stories. We observed this error only in stories predicted by GLACNet.

- **Description in Isolation:** Most sub-stories start with "This is a picture of...." Sentences of this nature sound more like single image captions than contextual stories.

- **Singular/Plural Disagreement:** The same story has one sentence with a singular noun and another sentence with the same noun but in plural form.

- **Ghost Entities:** Some sub-stories make use of a pronoun that has no antecedent at all (e.g., referring to a new person who was not introduced formally in the preceding sub-stories). This leads to confusion.

- **Personification:** The attribution of human-like qualities to something non-human due to lack of common sense knowledge.

- **Absurdity:** Nonsensical stories or sub-stories.

- **Incomplete Stories:** Stories that have less than 5 sentences.

- **Point-of-View Inconsistency:** The narrative point of view randomly changes within the story (e.g., first person to second person), creating confusion.

- **Excessive Paraphrasing:** Presence of sub-stories that have similar meanings but are expressed using different words or phrases.

We provide examples of each of the above error types in Table 3. In addition to analyzing errors in stories with low predictions, we uncovered several anomalies in stories with high predictions. We provide examples of these in Table 4.

6.2   Discussion

The most common error types we observed were repetitions and descriptions in isolation; we present statistics indicating the frequencies of

Error Type	Example
Grammatical Errors	*there was a lot of people at the convention center* . we saw a lot of interesting signs . there were a lot of people there . there were a lot of people there . we had a great time at the bar . (AREL)
	the man was taking a walk on the sidewalk . he saw a lot of cool buildings . he saw a statue of a woman . *he was a big group of people* . he went to the museum . (GLACNet)
Contradictions	we went to the art gallery . we saw a lot of people there . *the streets were empty . the streets were full of people* . this is a picture of a woman . (AREL)
Repetitions within Story	*the bride and groom were very happy to be married* . the bride and groom were so happy to be married . *the bride and groom were so happy to be married* . we all had a great time at the reception . they danced the night away . (AREL)
	the family went to the zoo . they had a lot of fun . they were all very excited . *we had a great time . i had a great time* . (Contextualize, Show and Tell)
Repetitions within Sent.	it was a beautiful day for a trip to the beach . we took a trip to the beach . we went to the beach . the beach was beautiful . as *the sun went down , the sun went down* . (AREL)
Repetitive Subject	the water was calm and clear . the buildings were empty . the building was very tall . *the architecture was amazing . the architecture was breathtaking* . (GLACNet)
Repetitive Sentence Structure	the city is very beautiful . the bridge is amazing . the water is so nice . the ferris wheel is very good . the view is spectacular . (GLACNet)
Description in Isolation	*this is a picture of a street* . it was a long drive . there was a lot of damage to the side of the road . *this is a picture of a man* . after that we found a trail that was in the middle of the forest . (BLEU-RL)
	the flowers were very pretty the flowers were so beautiful . the flowers were beautiful . *this is a picture of a column* . it was a very nice place to be .(Contextualize, Show and Tell)
Singular/Plural Disagreement	the resort was beautiful . *the beach was nice . the beaches were amazing* . the water was so calm . the food was delicious . (GLACNet)
Ghost Entities	the lady was smiling for the camera . she was excited to be there . she was having a good time . *she was so happy to see **her*** . she was looking at the car (GLACNet)
Personification	*the plane was very excited to be at the location* . the first stop was the train station . the guide was also impressed with the organization organization . the students were able to see the exhibits from the city . the entire group was so happy to be there . (GLACNet)
Absurdity	*the kitchen was a lot of work . here is a picture of a box . i had to take a picture of my work . we had to take a picture of the menu . i had a great time* . (AREL)
	i bought a new car . this is a picture of a cat . she was very excited . and i 'm so excited . this is my favorite gift . (GLACNet)
Incomplete Stories	i love to travel i had a great time . she is having a great time . we went to the city to see some of the people . i had a great time . (AREL)
Point-of-View Inconsistency	*i was so excited to be graduating today . he was very proud of his graduation* . graduation day is always a success . he was very proud of his accomplishments . he was very proud of his accomplishments . (AREL)
Excessive Paraphrasing	we went on a trip to location . there were a lot of interesting things to see . there *were many different kinds of* fruits and vegetables . there *was also a variety of* fruits and vegetables . i had a great time there . (AREL)
	we took the kids to the park . *we had a lot of fun . we had a great time* . the kids were having a great time . we had a great time . (Contextualize, Show and Tell)

Table 3: Example stories associated with each error category. We identify the system that predicted each example in parentheses, and indicate the specific component of the story in error in italics when applicable.

these errors for AREL, GLACNet, and Contextualize, Show and Tell in Table 5 (note that both occurred with the highest frequency in AREL). The rarest error category was that containing incomplete stories. This error appeared only in AREL stories, and only in three of the 1010 generated stories (0.003%).

The prevalence of repetitions in AREL is likely a side-effect of the model's architecture—it generates the sub-stories for the whole album in parallel, rather than keeping track of what was generated in the previous sub-story. We found that this structure also led to some stories having contradictory sentences. In contrast, GLACNet stories exhibited

few repetitions because of the post-processing step employed after decoding. In this step, words for a sentence are sampled from a word probability distribution one hundred times and the most frequent word is selected. The words which occur in the generated sentences are also counted and the selection probabilities of words are decreased as their frequency increases.

It is somewhat surprising that the stories generated using Contextualize, Show and Tell also exhibited such a high frequency of repetitions, in spite of the fact that the model generated sub-stories sequentially. This demonstrates that some sort of feedback mechanism incorporating

Anom.	Example	Scores
Good Story, Low Score	we went to a halloween party . there were a lot of interesting things to see . we saw a lot of cool things . we saw a lot of old buildings . the christmas tree was the best part of the day . (AREL)	CIDEr: 4.27, BLEU-4: 0.00, BLEU-3: 15.79, BLEU-2: 29.76, BLEU-1: 50.95, ROUGE-L: 24.43, METEOR: 24.42
Bad Story, High Score	the couple was excited to be on vacation . they were going to the mountains . they went down the road . they saw a beautiful church . they had a nice dinner . (GLACNet)	CIDEr: 0.62
	the group of friends decided to go on a trip . they saw many interesting things . they stopped at a local restaurant . they had a great time . they ended up buying a new car . (GLACNet)	METEOR: 19.52, Bleu-4: 0.00, Bleu-3: 8.93, Bleu-2: 16.00, ROUGE-L: 22.55
	i went to a wedding last week . i had to take a picture of this beautiful flower . this is a picture of a woman . the flowers were so beautiful . the flowers were so beautiful . (AREL)	CIDEr: 20.90, Bleu-1: 71.79, Bleu-2: 43.47, METEOR: 33.98

Table 4: Example scoring anomalies, including the anomalous scores assigned to each story.

the model's previously generated sub-stories is needed. The output of each of the five decoders in Contextualize, Show and Tell should be fed into the next decoder to keep track of previously generated sub-stories.

We observed that there were very few grammatical errors in the GLACNet stories, as the probabilities associated with function words (e.g., prepositions and pronouns) remained unchanged even if their rate of occurrence was high. In contrast, stories generated by AREL (which includes no such grammar-checking mechanism) included a considerable number of grammatical errors. GLACNet's post-processing step still could be improved upon—we were somewhat surprised to find that some of its stories used both singular and plural forms of the same noun within a story. We assume the error occurred due to the fact that the model decreases the probability of frequently occurring words. Thus, if the singular noun occurred in the previous sub-story, its plural form gets included in the next sub-story.

The within-sentence repetitions may at least

Error Category	AREL-s-50	GLAC-Net	Contextualize, Show and Tell
Repetition of Sub-Stories	19.70%	2.08%	15.42%
Description in Isolation	29.01%	0%	15.79%

Table 5: Frequency (in terms of overall percentage) of the most common error types across all 1010 generated test stories by AREL and GLACNet and 1938 generated test stories by Contextualize, Show and Tell.

partially be a consequence of the presence of repetitions in some VIST training stories. In our analysis of the crowdsourced dataset we found that human typing/grammar errors were a relatively common occurrence, resulting in imperfect training data. Although the stories generated by GLACNet did not often exhibit repetitions due to the reasons mentioned in the paragraph above, there was a trade-off in terms of originality of the generated stories. We found that most were monotonous, using similar sentence structures for every story.

Descriptions in isolation, the single most prevalent error type we identified in AREL and Contextualize, Show and Tell stories, read more like image captions (describing the image's contents) than components of a sequential story. We are perplexed as to why these errors were so common, since to the best of our understanding the models did not include any DII instances in their training sets. It may be the case that caption-like sub-stories are learned to be "safer" choices by these models, and thus generated more often than riskier contextual sub-stories.

Sentences that are lexically different but semantically similar cause redundancies in the story and are a common occurrence in both GLACNet and AREL. Since images in a sequential album are often visually similar to one another, it may be the case that both models predict that two (or more) images in a sequence refer to the same content. In attempting to vary the resulting sub-stories nonetheless, they succeed only at generating paraphrases of one another.

7 Recommendations

As evidenced by our error analysis, there is substantial scope for improvement in visual storytelling. Based on our observations, we make the following recommendations. First, **automatically preprocessing the DII and SIS training files**

remains an unexplored but potentially highly useful preliminary step in the story generation process. Doing so could aid future systems in avoiding grammatical mistakes, particularly if coupled with a post-processing mechanism similar to what is currently employed by GLACNet. Second, in terms of the post-processing mechanism itself, **incorporating temporal sequencing methods will yield more well-organized and coherent stories**. This could be done by sorting a (presumably jumbled) set of sub-stories after they have been generated, as was done by Agrawal et al. (2016).

Third, it is common for current models to generate all sub-stories in parallel. This leads to repetitions and redundancies in the generated stories. **Modifying the architecture in such a way that the sub-stories are generated sequentially and the word tokens of the previously generated sub-stories are passed back to the model may lead to numerous benefits.** For instance, this feedback could be used to identify past sub-story topics, as well as to ensure that the singularity/plurality of subjects remains the same across the entire story. Incorporating a memory mechanism could also lessen the frequency of point-of-view inconsistencies, excessive paraphrasing, and contradictions. The architecture of the decoder used by Venugopalan et al. (2015) can also be adopted for providing feedback at the word level along with the sub-story level feedback. This will help in keeping track of the previously generated words in the story and prevent in-sentence repetitions.

Fourth, **traditional image captions (DIIs) can be (carefully) leveraged to support the generation of high-quality stories**, for instance by facilitating named entity recognition and thereby decreasing the frequency of ghost entities. Another way to avoid ghost entities is to (fifth) **incorporate a bottom-up and top-down visual attention mechanism**, such as that used in prior image captioning work (Anderson et al., 2018), to learn image-specific features and facilitate visual grounding. Few-shot learning methods to jointly encode the images and text (Dong et al., 2018) could also be used in this regard.

Sixth, although Jain et al.'s (2017) work considered only textual features, **a machine translation model could be used** to produce more creative stories while avoiding repetitive sentence structures and absurdities to some degree. Matusov et al. (2017) use a neural machine translation model which contains a visual encoder and a textual encoder, thus giving attention independently to both image features and source sentences. This technique is a more viable option. Finally, the anomalies we uncovered in our error analysis validate the position first put forward by Wang et al. (2018), that automatic metrics leave much to be desired in terms of judging visual storytelling approaches. We recommend that a standardized human evaluation metric be included in the assessment of these approaches in the future.

8 Conclusion

In this work, we conduct a comprehensive error analysis of recent visual storytelling approaches. We note current shortcomings in this area, and make recommendations for addressing these limitations in future work. We find that the most common errors are repetitions, the presence of traditional image descriptions, and a lack of creativity in the machine-generated stories. Preprocessing the training text, developing a combined visual and text co-attention mechanism, and sequentially generating sub-stories and providing them as feedback to the model could all help to ameliorate these issues. Specifically, including these elements could help in the generation of more context-aware sequential sub-stories, and temporally sequencing the sub-stories will produce more creative, coherent, relevant, and most importantly, humanlike stories. We plan to experiment with the techniques mentioned above in our future work.

Acknowledgements

We thank the anonymous reviewers for their comments and suggestions. This material is based upon work supported by Google Cloud.

References

Harsh Agrawal, Arjun Chandrasekaran, Dhruv Batra, Devi Parikh, and Mohit Bansal. 2016. Sort story: Sorting jumbled images and captions into stories. In *Proceedings of the 2016 Conference on Empirical Methods in Natural Language Processing*, pages 925–931, Austin, Texas. Association for Computational Linguistics.

Peter Anderson, Xiaodong He, Chris Buehler, Damien Teney, Mark Johnson, Stephen Gould, and Lei Zhang. 2018. Bottom-up and top-down attention for image captioning and visual question answering. In *Proceedings of the IEEE Conference on Computer Vision and Pattern Recognition*, pages 6077–6086.

Satanjeev Banerjee and Alon Lavie. 2005. Meteor: An automatic metric for mt evaluation with improved correlation with human judgments. In *Proceedings of the ACL Workshop on Intrinsic and Extrinsic Evaluation Measures for Machine Translation and/or Summarization*, pages 65–72, Ann Arbor. Association for Computational Linguistics.

Xuanyi Dong, Linchao Zhu, De Zhang, Yi Yang, and Fei Wu. 2018. Fast parameter adaptation for few-shot image captioning and visual question answering. In *Proceedings of the 2018 ACM on Multimedia Conference (ACM MM)*.

Diana Gonzalez-Rico and Gibran Fuentes Pineda. 2018. Contextualize, show and tell: A neural visual storyteller. *CoRR*, abs/1806.00738.

Kaiming He, Xiangyu Zhang, Shaoqing Ren, and Jian Sun. 2016. Deep residual learning for image recognition. In *2016 IEEE Conference on Computer Vision and Pattern Recognition, CVPR 2016, Las Vegas, NV, USA, June 27-30, 2016*, pages 770–778.

Chao-Chun Hsu, Szu-Min Chen, Ming-Hsun Hsieh, and Lun-Wei Ku. 2018. Using inter-sentence diverse beam search to reduce redundancy in visual storytelling. *CoRR*, abs/1805.11867.

Ting-Hao (Kenneth) Huang, Francis Ferraro, Nasrin Mostafazadeh, Ishan Misra, Aishwarya Agrawal, Jacob Devlin, Ross Girshick, Xiaodong He, Pushmeet Kohli, Dhruv Batra, C. Lawrence Zitnick, Devi Parikh, Lucy Vanderwende, Michel Galley, and Margaret Mitchell. 2016. Visual storytelling. In *Proceedings of the 2016 Conference of the North American Chapter of the Association for Computational Linguistics: Human Language Technologies*, pages 1233–1239. Association for Computational Linguistics.

Parag Jain, Priyanka Agrawal, Abhijit Mishra, Mohak Sukhwani, Anirban Laha, and Karthik Sankaranarayanan. 2017. Story generation from sequence of independent short descriptions. In *Proceedings of the KDD Workshop on Machine Learning for Creativity*.

Taehyeong Kim, Min-Oh Heo, Seonil Son, Kyoung-Wha Park, and Byoung-Tak Zhang. 2018. GLAC net: Glocal attention cascading networks for multi-image cued story generation. *CoRR*, abs/1805.10973.

S. Kullback and R. A. Leibler. 1951. On information and sufficiency. *The Annals of Mathematical Statistics*, 22(1):79–86.

Chin-Yew Lin and Franz Josef Och. 2004. Automatic evaluation of machine translation quality using longest common subsequence and skip-bigram statistics. In *Proceedings of the 42nd Meeting of the Association for Computational Linguistics (ACL'04), Main Volume*, pages 605–612, Barcelona, Spain.

Tsung-Yi Lin, Michael Maire, Serge Belongie, James Hays, Pietro Perona, Deva Ramanan, Piotr Dollár, and C. Lawrence Zitnick. 2014. Microsoft coco: Common objects in context. In *Computer Vision – ECCV 2014*, pages 740–755, Cham. Springer International Publishing.

Stephanie Lukin, Reginald Hobbs, and Clare Voss. 2018. A pipeline for creative visual storytelling. In *Proceedings of the First Workshop on Storytelling*, pages 20–32. Association for Computational Linguistics.

Mitchell P. Marcus, Beatrice Santorini, and Mary Ann Marcinkiewicz. 1993. Building a large annotated corpus of english: The penn treebank. *Computational Linguistics*, 19(2).

Evgeny Matusov, Andy Way, Iacer Calixto, Daniel Stein, Pintu Lohar, and Sheila Castilho. 2017. Using images to improve machine-translating e-commerce product listings. In *Proceedings of the 15th Conference of the European Chapter of the Association for Computational Linguistics, EACL 2017, Valencia, Spain, April 3-7, 2017, Volume 2: Short Papers*, pages 637–643.

Kishore Papineni, Salim Roukos, Todd Ward, and Wei-Jing Zhu. 2002. Bleu: a method for automatic evaluation of machine translation. In *Proceedings of 40th Annual Meeting of the Association for Computational Linguistics*, pages 311–318, Philadelphia, Pennsylvania, USA. Association for Computational Linguistics.

Olga Russakovsky, Jia Deng, Hao Su, Jonathan Krause, Sanjeev Satheesh, Sean Ma, Zhiheng Huang, Andrej Karpathy, Aditya Khosla, Michael Bernstein, Alexander C. Berg, and Li Fei-Fei. 2015. ImageNet Large Scale Visual Recognition Challenge. *International Journal of Computer Vision (IJCV)*, 115(3):211–252.

C. Szegedy, V. Vanhoucke, S. Ioffe, J. Shlens, and Z. Wojna. 2016. Rethinking the inception architecture for computer vision. In *2016 IEEE Conference on Computer Vision and Pattern Recognition (CVPR)*, pages 2818–2826, Los Alamitos, CA, USA. IEEE Computer Society.

R. Vedantam, C. L. Zitnick, and D. Parikh. 2015. Cider: Consensus-based image description evaluation. In *2015 IEEE Conference on Computer Vision and Pattern Recognition (CVPR)*, pages 4566–4575.

Subhashini Venugopalan, Marcus Rohrbach, Jeff Donahue, Raymond J. Mooney, Trevor Darrell, and Kate Saenko. 2015. Sequence to sequence - video to text. *CoRR*, abs/1505.00487.

Xin Wang, Wenhu Chen, Yuan-Fang Wang, and William Yang Wang. 2018. No metrics are perfect: Adversarial reward learning for visual storytelling. In *Proceedings of the 56th Annual Meeting of the Association for Computational Linguistics (Volume 1: Long Papers)*, pages 899–909. Association for Computational Linguistics.

Licheng Yu, Mohit Bansal, and Tamara Berg. 2017. Hierarchically-attentive rnn for album summarization and storytelling. In *Proceedings of the 2017 Conference on Empirical Methods in Natural Language Processing*, pages 966–971, Copenhagen, Denmark. Association for Computational Linguistics.

"Caption" as a Coherence Relation: Evidence and Implications

Malihe Alikhani
Computer Science
Rutgers University
malihe.alikhani@rutgers.edu

Matthew Stone
Computer Science
Rutgers University
matthew.stone@rutgers.edu

Abstract

We study verbs in image–text corpora, contrasting *caption* corpora, where texts are explicitly written to characterize image content, with *depiction* corpora, where texts and images may stand in more general relations. Captions show a distinctively limited distribution of verbs, with strong preferences for specific tense, aspect, lexical aspect, and semantic field. These limitations, which appear in data elicited by a range of methods, restrict the utility of caption corpora to inform image retrieval, multimodal document generation, and perceptually-grounded semantic models. We suggest that these limitations reflect the discourse constraints in play when subjects write texts to accompany imagery, so we argue that future development of image–text corpora should work to increase the diversity of event descriptions, while looking explicitly at the different ways text and imagery can be coherently related.

1 Introduction

Researchers interested in modeling relations between language and the world are increasingly starting from multimodal corpora that combine text with visual information; see Bernardi et al. (2017) for review.

A key benchmark problem, which we explore here, is to learn to produce an appropriate text caption to accompany an image. This problem brings fundamental scientific and engineering challenges, and has immediate applications, particularly in making online content more accessible. At the same time, the problem lends itself to appealing high-level characterizations—learning to describe in words what's happening in an image—which suggests that the line of research affords sweeping insights into depiction, image retrieval, and real-world commonsense inference.

In this paper, we offer a theoretically-situated but empirically-motivated critique of this broader understanding of captioning. We argue that current image–caption corpora systematically suffer from key deficits in coverage, and therefore cannot underpin general models for linking images and text. Instead, we suggest that these deficits might be remedied through attention to different corpora and different image–text relationships.

Our starting point is the observation that images and text in multimodal documents are used coherently together: like all contributions to discourse, they stand in particular relations to one another, which guide readers toward the inferential connections intended by the author (Hobbs, 1990). **Captioning**, we argue, is such a relation. A text that is presented as the caption to an image presents restricted kinds of information about the image and adopts a distinctive perspective. In particular, we suggest, captions characteristically describe imagery as though what we see has been going on indefinitely in the past, is happening now, and will continue indefinitely into the future.

We justify this account of captioning with an empirical study of action descriptions in English image captioning corpora. Our central finding is that they are disproportionately **atelic**, meaning that they describe an ongoing process in a general way, without invoking its possible goal, endpoint or culmination; see Hamm and Bott (2018). This is the difference between *painting an advertisement* (telic) and *using oils* (atelic); *performing their hit song* (telic) and *performing on stage* (atelic); *running a 5K* (telic) and simply *running* (atelic). Of course, captions frequently feature **stative** descriptions, which evoke conditions rather than activities: *names are etched on a wall, the building towers over the skyline.*

Captioning is just one of many possible coherence relations connecting text and imagery: we

Proceedings of the Second Workshop on Shortcomings in Vision and Language, pages 58–67
Minneapolis, USA, June 6, 2019. ©2017 Association for Computational Linguistics

(a) People are standing outside next to a food truck.

(b) A man is sitting in front of a bunch of fruit.

(c) It was a beautiful day for him.

(d) Actor and guest arrive at the premiere.

(e) Score small X at base of each peach with paring knife.

(f) Lower peaches into boiling water and simmer until skins loosen, 30 to 60 seconds.

Figure 1: The difference in instruction results in different captions. People take a particular perspective when writing captions. (a) and (b) are examples from COCO. (c) shows one step of a story in VIST. (d) is an example from the Google caption dataset. (e) and (f) are examples of two steps of a multimodal recipe.
Photo credits: (a) by Gary Soup, (b) by Carol Mitchell, (c) by Jeff Kravitz/FilmMagic/GettyImages, (e) and (f) by Kate Kelly/AmericasTestKitchen.

can find diverse relations considering a broader range of corpus data. Figure 1 illustrates these possibilities. Figure 1(a) and (b), from MSCOCO (Lin et al., 2014), are typical descriptive examples from caption data sets, describing imagery in terms of open-ended activities. Figure 1(c), from (Huang et al., 2016), and (d), from (Sharma et al., 2018), exhibit another possibility: these images are accompanied by **play-by-play text**, written in the narrative present (Pullum et al., 2002, 129), which suggests that the photo catches the moment that makes the captions true. Many other cases, we argue, are best analyzed in terms of an **illustration** relation connecting text to an accompanying image. As shown in Figure 1(e) and (f), from (Yagcioglu et al., 2018), illustration relations allow for diverse verbs—telic, atelic and stative alike—to be described in the text.

Thus, where vision–language applications in-

volve this illustration relation, as is plausible in many cases of image retrieval, document synthesis, and grounded language use, caption corpora will systematically lack the full range of action descriptions that general solutions must handle. We conclude by arguing that future researchers should focus on naturally-occurring examples, where text and images connect in diverse ways, and should explicitly model the coherence relationships between text and images.

2 Related Work

Vision–language corpora have inspired a range of approaches for image retrieval and language generation, and increasing awareness of the biases of corpora and models is bringing increased attention to the linguistic characteristics of the corpora (Bernardi et al., 2017; Ferraro et al., 2015). For example, van Miltenburg et al. (2018a) present a tax-

K	COCO	Flickr	VIST	CC	Recipe	ANC
Top 10	0.599	0.594	0.538	0.390	0.392	0.443
Top 30	0.724	0.723	0.669	0.535	0.511	0.563
Top 100	0.864	0.840	0.822	0.834	0.715	0.709
Top 300	0.948	0.934	0.920	0.930	0.862	0.840

Table 1: Fraction of verbal part-of-speech tokens accounted for by top K verb lemmas, by corpus. Frequent verbs disproportionately dominate in captions.

onomy of the ways that subjects refer to people in the images, while van Miltenburg et al. (2018b) investigate the difference between spoken and written image descriptions. We continue this trend by offering a comparative study of verb use in multimodal corpora for the first time.

Authors intend contributions to play specific roles in multimodal discourse. Previous works characterized the inferences that guide interpretations between images in terms of coherence relations (McCloud, 1993; Cohn, 2013; Cumming et al., 2017). In this work, we explore relations between images and text, with a particular emphasis on the link between images and captions.

Gella et al. (2019) presented a model for disambiguating verb senses in images (e.g. playing guitar v.s. children playing) using a single verb and the related image as the inputs of the system. Our work is different because we are investigating how people write captions for images and not a single verb.

We investigate the relationship between tense, aspect and discourse structure in image–text corpora. This will naturally raise the question of whether we can distinguish between what information is in an image caption and how that relates to existing verb classes. We draw on existing verb classifications to capture lexical and grammatical aspects for our empirical study. (Vendler, 1957; Levin, 1993; Baker et al., 1998; Schuler, 2005; Dowty, 1986; Comrie, 1976; Krifka, 1998).

3 Method

We study five prominent image–text corpora that vary in how constrained the relationship is between image and text:

- Microsoft Common Objects in Context (COCO) (Lin et al., 2014);
- Flickr30K (Flickr) (Young et al., 2014);
- Visual Storytelling (VIST) (Huang et al., 2016);

- Google's Conceptual Captions (CC) (Sharma et al., 2018); and
- the Recipe dataset (Yagcioglu et al., 2018).

COCO, Flickr and VIST are crowdsourced corpora, while CC and the Recipe dataset collect user-generated text. These corpora are designed to focus on the captioning relations exhibited in Figure 1. VIST asks for descriptive texts to link five images into a short narrative; CC pairs web images with relevant text from associated ALT-TEXT HTML attributes. These corpora may exhibit a broader range of inferential connections between image in text, such as the cases of play-by-play narrative in Figure 1. Finally, the Recipe dataset collects naturally-occurring text and images developed in combination, and includes a wide range of illustration relations (and a range of other strategies for achieving coherence across modalities which offer possibilities for future research).

To assess what's distinctive about these corpora, we compare them to two points of reference: the American National Corpus (ANC) which is a balanced corpus of spoken and written English (Leech et al., 2014) and Facebook's children's stories (FS) (Hill et al., 2015), a corpus of written narrative.

To measure different verb forms, we used part-of-speech tags, parses, and dependency labels, computed using the SpaCy natural language processing toolkit (Honnibal and Johnson, 2015), to find verbs and their associated auxiliaries. We then applied rules to classify the verb groups into past or non-past forms (including present, modal, and non-finite forms), and separately into simple (e.g., *ran*), progressive (e.g., *was running*) or perfect aspect (e.g., *has run*). Perfect progressive forms (*has been running*) are classed with perfect, since they share the focus on a result state not an ongoing activity. We keep a separate count for **copular** (copula) forms of the verb *be*—those that relate a subject to a predicate expressed as a noun phrase, adjective phrase or prepositional phrase.

4 The Simplicity of Caption Corpora

We begin with the overall finding that motivates our research: Verb use in image–caption corpora is markedly rarer and less diverse than in ANC.

Verbs are less frequent overall in image–caption corpora. In ANC, 0.184 of the tokens have verb POS tags; that drops to 0.065 in CC, 0.026 in COCO, 0.017 in VIST and 0.012 in Flickr. (The difference seems wild, but remember captions won't have helper verbs for modals, passive, and negation, and may be bare noun phrases.) But the frequency of verbs also drops off faster in image–caption corpora, particularly across the most frequent 100 verbs. Table 1 shows how strongly the top 10 and top 30 lemmas dominate in image–caption corpora. By comparison, image–text data sets that allow for more varied links between images and text, particularly the Recipe dataset, show more diverse verb usage. This suggests that it's not just the connection between text and image that limits verb use, but the particular constraints of caption content.

Looking at the frequent verbs from Flickr and COCO gives a sense of the uniformity of captions. The 17 Frequent Caption Verbs listed in Table 2

is/are	wearing	sitting	standing
has/have	walking	holding	looking
playing	jumping	watching	smiling
talking	doing	eating	carrying
running	driving	laying	

Table 2: Verbs occurring at least 100 times per million words in COCO (Lin et al., 2014) or Flickr (Young et al., 2014), shown in their most frequent forms: *be* and *have* (simple present), plus 17 verbs we call the Frequent Caption Verbs (FCVs) (present participle).

make up 40.4% of verbs in COCO but only 6.30% of verbs in AN (not counting *be*, 23.3% of ANC and 23.0% of COCO; or *have*, 6.5% of ANC and 2.8% of COCO). Note how almost all the FCVs involve sustained activities associated with distinctive poses.

Not surprisingly, similar vocabulary is found in image captioning systems trained on these data sets. Table 3 tabulates the kinds of verbs produced across the COCO development set by eight successful image captioning models (Dai et al., 2017; Tavakoli et al., 2017; Liu et al., 2017; Mun et al.,

2017). We can see that the outputs of these models also exhibit a preponderance of descriptions with FCVs and *be/have*.

models	FCVs	be/have	other
Dai et al., 2017	0.572	0.231	0.197
Liu et al., 2017	0.571	0.271	0.158
Mun et al., 2017	0.638	0.266	0.095
Tavakoli et al., 2017	0.609	0.231	0.160
Shetty et al., 2016	0.535	0.282	0.183
Shetty et al., 2017	0.609	0.231	0.160
Zhou et al., 2017	0.609	0.256	0.135
Wu et al., 2017	0.561	0.257	0.181

Table 3: Relative frequency of different kinds of verbs produced by eight captioning models trained on COCO.

5 Properties of Captions

Why are the verbs of captions so impoverished? The commonalities of the verbs in Table 2 suggests that it's because captions present specific kinds of information, in characteristic ways. We hypothesize that these constraints are associated with a **Caption** coherence relation that authors can use to link image and text into a coherent whole. In this section, we identify key semantic and pragmatic properties of this Caption relation.

Caption verbs show morphological commonalities: *ing*-forms predominate, which suggests that caption writers prefer progressive aspect, describing events as ongoing throughout some topic time—here, presumably, the moment of the photo. The progressive form combines with the auxiliary *be*: the predominance of *is* and *are* over *was* and *were* indicates that caption writers prefer present tense descriptions, construing the moment of the photo as "now" that anchors the speaker's perspective. Section 5.1 confirms that these are distinctive and characteristic features specifically cued by captioning tasks.

Caption verbs also show semantic commonalities. Not surprisingly, all involve visible events; Section 5.2 quantifies this preference. In addition, the verbs generally either are stative or describe unbounded activities without an inherent culmination or end-point; this is known in linguistics as atelic aktionsart (Vendler, 1957; Verkuyl, 2005). Section 5.3 reports an analysis confirming that captions prefer atelic descriptions over telic ones.

	progressive	perfect	simple	copula	past	non-past
COCO	0.493	0.121	0.193	0.187	0.140	0.850
Flickr	0.481	0.065	0.208	0.339	0.120	0.879
VIST	0.112	0.081	0.702	0.104	0.517	0.482
CC	0.207	0.161	0.528	0.103	0.139	0.860
Recipe	0.121	0.109	0.667	0.103	0.219	0.781
ANC	0.075	0.188	0.621	0.109	0.403	0.592
FS	0.076	0.126	0.647	0.137	0.606	0.382

Table 4: Grammatical tense and aspect across corpora. Progressive and non-past dominate in Flickr and COCO whereas the simple form dominates in Recipe, ANC and FS. The dataset from the image–text corpora that is the closest to ANC with respect to aspect is the Recipe dataset.

Overall then, we conclude that Caption texts offer present-tense descriptions anchored to the moment depicted in the related image and appeal to temporally unbounded eventualities to summarize the information explicitly visible in that image.

5.1 Captions prefer present progressive

We report the percentages of realization of tense and aspect on verbs that project full sentences across corpora in Table 4. Progressive verbs make 49% and 48% of COCO and Flickr respectively. The linguistic expressions in these captions mainly include reference to here and now, describing the situation in a progressive form. ANC on the other hand, includes only around 8% progressive verbs. For all the pairs, the distributions of tense and aspect are reliably different ($\chi^2 > 39.03$, $p < 0.04$).

COCO and Flickr show a preponderance of progressive and non-past forms. The effect is even larger in the results of the models that are trained on COCO. As we can see in Table 5 progressive form makes up to 74% of the output of the models. Note that we know from Table 3 that these models have between 23% to 28% *be* and *have*.

models	non-past	progressive
Dai et al.,2017	0.994	0.550
Liu et al.,2017	0.995	0.709
Mun et al.,2017	0.998	0.691
Tavakoli et al.,2017	0.999	0.731
Shetty et al.,2016	0.998	0.728
Shetty et al.,2017	0.992	0.519
Zhou et al., 2017	0.998	0.739
Wu et al., 2017	0.998	0.678

Table 5: Relative frequency of non-past and progressive in verbs produced by eight captioning models trained on COCO.

CC shows a greatly increased use of simple forms in the present, while VIST shows simple forms in a mix of present and past. The instructions in VIST to tell a story, and the genre conventions of ALT-TEXT, lead to play-by-play descriptions in the narrative present (or sometimes for VIST, past) rather than the progressive descriptions provided by crowd-workers who just describe what they see.

Table 4 shows that VIST has a different distribution of tense and aspect in comparison to FS. Overall, FS includes 10% more past verbs. This involves more past perfect and simple past verbs where VIST includes more present progressive and simple present.

5.2 Captions prefer visible event verbs

Caption verbs also show semantic commonalities. Not surprisingly, they tend to involve visible events; that rules out a rich array of verbs that generally occur frequently.

To quantify this, we counted the occurrences of verbs in five Levin classes (Levin, 1993): desire verbs (e.g. need, want), verbs of psychological states (e.g. cheer, worry), declare verbs (e.g. believe, suppose), learn verbs (e.g. learn, memorize) and conceal verbs (e.g. screen, hide). The complete list can be found in the appendix. These verbs occur with a frequency of more than 20 per thousand words in ANC. They occur just 10.2, 15.7 and 16.6 times per million words in COCO, Flickr and VIST respectively. The differences are stark: even in telling a story, crowd workers confine themselves to the imagery, and stick to the visible facts. Other genres are less constrained; we find these verbs in CC and Recipe at a rate of 1080 and 1087 per million. Anecdotally, this reflects the additional relations that can link images and text

A black frisbee is sitting on top of a roof.	A man playing soccer outside of a white house with a red door.	The boy is throwing a soccer ball by the red door.	A soccer ball is over a roof by a frisbee in a rain gutter.	Two balls and a frisbee are on top of a roof.
A discus got stuck up on the roof.	Why not try getting it down with a soccer ball?	Up the soccer ball goes.	It didn't work so we tried a volley ball.	Now the discus, soccer ball, and volleyball are all stuck on the roof.

Table 6: An example from VIST dataset that illustrates the difference between descriptive captions (middle row) and narrative (bottom row) and different uses of verbal tense and aspect in multimodal corpora. Photo credit: Ron Bieber

in these data sets. For example, ALT-TEXT fields often report first-person evaluations commenting on the imagery—prototypically, *I love it [what's shown]*, or *I want it [what's shown]*.

Do all visible verbs occur equally in image–text corpora? Of course not. Verbs differ in many different ways, most notably in their "image prior", how likely they are to happen during photo opportunities or to be featured and mentioned when images are published online. However, if someone says an event is common and interesting to watch and describe, but also says that it's rare to photograph it, you should be skeptical.

With that in mind, consider the verbs in Table 7. Truly invisible verbs, like *worry* and *wonder*, are not only missing from Flickr, COCO and VIST, but yield almost no hits on the web in the pattern *saw them V*. We also find frequent FCVs, like *walk* and *sit*, that occur widely across genres. The challenge are cases like *build* and *draw*. Google Ngram counts for *saw them build* and *saw them draw* confirm that they describe visible events with high frequency across text corpora, but these verbs are nevertheless rare in image–caption corpora. Maybe there's more to say here.

5.3 Captions prefer atelic descriptions

Our hypothesis is that the **lexical aspect** of verbs (Hamm and Bott, 2018) plays an important role in image captions. Lexical aspect describes the temporal structure of described eventualities. There are three main cases. **Stative** descriptions characterize ongoing conditions that do not involve dynamic activity, like *being* or *having*. **Atelic** ones characterize processes that can continue indefinitely, like *waiting* or *standing*. **Telic** ones characterize events that reach a definite endpoint and stop, like *arriving* or *winning*. What's relevant here is that a moment in time suffices to see that stative and atelic eventualities are under way. Telic descriptions can be established only by seeing the endpoint being realized, perhaps after an appropriate preparatory process.

Lexical aspect is partly due to the lexical meaning of the verb, but it also depends on whether relevant arguments are described in a delimited way or not—which gives rise to the linguistic problem of aspectual composition (Verkuyl, 2005). *Running* is an unbounded, atelic process. But *running the race* is a telic description: it ends when the race is run. And *running races* is again atelic: you can keep running new races indefinitely. The difference between telic and atelic descriptions thus has to be labeled by human annotators, based on the verb and its arguments.

If caption writers want to see the event they report, they should be reluctant to use telic descriptions. The image might not show the necessary culmination or the process leading up to it. However, this prediction depends on how speakers understand the progressive and narrative present forms. Semanticists often argue—on the basis of true examples like *In the '70s, Jodorowsky was making a film of "Dune" [but he never finished it]*—that a telic progressive description should be understood as a generic description of ongoing activities, **not** as a prediction of an eventual outcome. This is known as the imperfective paradox.

		worry	wonder	walk	sit	build	draw
corpus frequency	Flickr	0.1	0.4	524.6	675.0	10.4	10.5
	COCO	0.1	0.1	683.5	1991.5	3.2	2.1
	VIST	9.8	2.3	130.9	64.3	14.6	7.2
	CC	0	76.9	1745.6	1273.5	417.2	395.2
	ANC	143.6	196.1	264.4	269.1	323.6	167.5
Google Ngram	made them V	374	1975	2071	6121	919	1444
	saw them V	0	47	1586	412	193	713

Table 7: Corpus frequencies of select verbs (per million words) and counts from the Google Ngram dataset. The frequencies of *worry* and *wonder* are low in both image–text and the Google Ngram datasets. However, the frequencies of *build* and *draw*, while low in image–text corpora, are high in the Google Ngram dataset.

(Hamm and Bott, 2018). If this is captioners' understanding, they should use progressive telic descriptions freely, whenever they offer the best description of the activities visible in the image.

We (the authors) together with an undergraduate linguistics major at Rutgers drew 500 captions parsed as sentences from all of the datasets and derived a consensus annotation of whether those descriptions are stative, atelic, or telic. Verbs in telic and atelic classes are labeled as punctual or durative events (Moens, 1987; King, 1969). [1]

To calculate the effect size (a proxy for the difference of proportions of telic verbs across two data sets) that we are able to detect with 500 samples, we performed a sensitivity power analysis. The result of the analysis suggests that with a sample size of 500, we are able to detect effects sizes as small as 0.1650 with a power and significance level of 95% (Faul et al., 2014).

	durative	punctual
Flickr	22	7
COCO	23	5
VIST	79	33
CC	45	59
Recipe	189	110
ANC	197	97

Table 8: Counts of telic verbs out of 500 randomly selected sentences from each dataset. Pairwise comparisons of datasets suggest that every datasets is significantly different from others with the exception of two pairs; COCO and Flickr as well as Recipe and ANC. In general, the caption corpora contain fewer telic verbs in comparison to ANC and Recipe.

Table 8 presents the results of the annotation task. The results of t-test and f-test confirm that

image–caption corpora emphasize atelic descriptions. For CC, noisy text meant our sample included only 412 relevant items, giving a telic rate of 0.252. In particular, an f-test shows that the distributions of telic verbs in these corpora are different ($f = 409.8$, $p = 1.1e - 644$). By t-test, Flickr is similar to COCO ($t = 0.12$, $p = 0.890$) and Recipe is similar to ANC ($t = -0.90, p = 0.366$), but all other datasets are two by two significantly different ($t>10$, $p < 0.0001$).

To calculate the inter-rater agreement, we determined Cohen's κ. We randomly selected 200 sentences from CC and assigned each to two annotators. The κ is 0.77, which indicates substantial agreement (Viera et al., 2005).

Our analysis depends on aspectual composition. In Flickr and COCO, FCVs contribute to atelic descriptions in 96% of occurrences whereas these verbs contribute to atelic descriptions only 39% of occurrences in ANC, because of different word senses and argument realizations. By contrast, verbs that contribute to telic descriptions in Flickr also contribute to telic descriptions in ANC in 98% of the cases. This underscores that the preference for atelic descriptions in image captions is a systematic phenomenon and not just an artifact of the small number of verbs found in the corpora.

6 Conclusions

By analyzing verb usage in image–caption corpora, we find that writers asked to caption an image take a particular perspective: they describe visible eventualities as present, continuing, and indefinite in temporal extent. These features help explain why verb use in captioning corpora is extremely limited—and these limitations persist in automatic captioning systems. We have offered a discourse perspective on these limitations, fol-

---

[1] The annotations are available at https://github.com/malihealikhani/Captions

lowing Hobbs (1990): a distinctive coherence relation governs the inferential and intentional relationships between images and caption text.

This is no slight to captions—they may well be challenging to model and useful to produce. However, this seems not to be the only kind of move that authors use to connect images and text. Broader corpora also feature play-by-play narrative, reactions and comments, illustrations, and perhaps other coherence relations between images and text. These relations deserve further study, but the preliminary evidence we have provided already suggests that these relations can accommodate a very different range of verbs than what's found in captions.

For now, the diversity of verb usage (and, perhaps, coherence relations) found in naturalistic image–text corpora like the Recipe dataset suggests some drawbacks for applying captioning models for novel applications. For example, consider using text as a cue for image retrieval: caption models might have good coverage for descriptions of extended activities that are clearly cued by people's pose, but they won't be very helpful for descriptions that characterize ongoing events in terms of their ultimate goal or outcome. This is not because those pictures are missing, because people aren't interested in seeing or describing those events, or because of the inherent limits of computer vision or semantic modeling techniques, but simply because the relevant descriptions happen to be missing from caption datasets, because of the conventions for writing coherent captions. We might well get better models by training on a broader range of data, including corpora where texts are accompanied by illustrations. Similarly, we can expect caption models to have limited utility in generating illustrated documents, as reported in one case by Ravi et al. (2018), because the vocabulary of events we might want to illustrate diverges so much from the vocabulary of captions.

We therefore recommend that future image–text corpora should explicitly look to explore and characterize the different ways text and imagery can be coherently related, including using the kinds of semantic and pragmatic analyses that we have presented here. A more inclusive collection effort should have the effect of increasing the diversity of event descriptions observed in image–text corpora, while laying the groundwork for more systematic coverage of applications. At the same time, our explorations have also revealed a clear need to improve theoretical and computational resources for verb classification to better characterize perceptual and temporal inference. So such efforts promise to refine theories of coherence and verb meaning in linguistics and cognitive science.

7   Acknowledgement

The research presented in this paper is supported by NSF Award IIS-1526723 and in part through a fellowship from the Rutgers Discovery Informatics Institute. Thanks to Divya Appasamy for helping us with the annotations. We are grateful for discussions and comments from Doug DeCarlo and Margaret Mitchell.

References

Collin F Baker, Charles J Fillmore, and John B Lowe. 1998. The berkeley framenet project. In *Proceedings of the 17th international conference on Computational linguistics-Volume 1*, pages 86–90. Association for Computational Linguistics.

Raffaella Bernardi, Ruket Çakici, Desmond Elliott, Aykut Erdem, Erkut Erdem, Nazli Ikizler-Cinbis, Frank Keller, Adrian Muscat, and Barbara Plank. 2017. Automatic description generation from images: A survey of models, datasets, and evaluation measures (extended abstract). In *Proceedings of the Twenty-Sixth International Joint Conference on Artificial Intelligence, IJCAI 2017, Melbourne, Australia, August 19-25, 2017*, pages 4970–4974.

Neil Cohn. 2013. Visual narrative structure. *Cognitive science*, 37(3):413–452.

Bernard Comrie. 1976. *Aspect: An introduction to the study of verbal aspect and related problems*, volume 2. Cambridge university press.

Samuel Cumming, Gabriel Greenberg, and Rory Kelly. 2017. Conventions of viewpoint coherence in film. *Philosophers' Imprint*, 17(1):1–29.

Bo Dai, Sanja Fidler, Raquel Urtasun, and Dahua Lin. 2017. Towards diverse and natural image descriptions via a conditional gan. In *The IEEE International Conference on Computer Vision (ICCV)*.

David R Dowty. 1986. The effects of aspectual class on the temporal structure of discourse: semantics or pragmatics? *Linguistics and philosophy*, 9(1):37–61.

F Faul, E Erdfelder, AG Lang, and A Buchner. 2014. G* power: statistical power analyses for windows and mac.

Francis Ferraro, Nasrin Mostafazadeh, Lucy Vanderwende, Jacob Devlin, Michel Galley, Margaret Mitchell, et al. 2015. A survey of current datasets for vision and language research. *arXiv preprint arXiv:1506.06833*.

Spandana Gella, Frank Keller, and Mirella Lapata. 2019. Disambiguating visual verbs. *IEEE transactions on pattern analysis and machine intelligence*, 41(2):311–322.

Friedrich Hamm and Oliver Bott. 2018. Tense and aspect. In Edward N. Zalta, editor, *The Stanford Encyclopedia of Philosophy*, fall 2018 edition. Metaphysics Research Lab, Stanford University.

Felix Hill, Antoine Bordes, Sumit Chopra, and Jason Weston. 2015. The goldilocks principle: Reading children's books with explicit memory representations. *arXiv preprint arXiv:1511.02301*.

Jerry R Hobbs. 1990. *Literature and cognition*. 21. Center for the Study of Language (CSLI).

Matthew Honnibal and Mark Johnson. 2015. An improved non-monotonic transition system for dependency parsing. In *Proceedings of the 2015 Conference on Empirical Methods in Natural Language Processing*, pages 1373–1378, Lisbon, Portugal. Association for Computational Linguistics.

Ting-Hao Kenneth Huang, Francis Ferraro, Nasrin Mostafazadeh, Ishan Misra, Aishwarya Agrawal, Jacob Devlin, Ross Girshick, Xiaodong He, Pushmeet Kohli, Dhruv Batra, et al. 2016. Visual storytelling. In *Proceedings of the 2016 Conference of the North American Chapter of the Association for Computational Linguistics: Human Language Technologies*, pages 1233–1239.

Harold V King. 1969. Punctual versus durative as covert categories 1. *Language Learning*, 19(3-4):185–190.

Manfred Krifka. 1998. The origins of telicity. In *Events and grammar*, pages 197–235. Springer.

Geoffrey Leech, Paul Rayson, et al. 2014. *Word frequencies in written and spoken English: Based on the British National Corpus*. Routledge.

Beth Levin. 1993. *English verb classes and alternations: A preliminary investigation*. University of Chicago press.

Tsung-Yi Lin, Michael Maire, Serge Belongie, James Hays, Pietro Perona, Deva Ramanan, Piotr Dollár, and C Lawrence Zitnick. 2014. Microsoft coco: Common objects in context. In *European conference on computer vision*, pages 740–755. Springer.

Chang Liu, Fuchun Sun, Changhu Wang, Feng Wang, and Alan Yuille. 2017. Mat: A multimodal attentive translator for image captioning. In *Proceedings of the Twenty-Sixth International Joint Conference on Artificial Intelligence, IJCAI-17*, pages 4033–4039.

Scott McCloud. 1993. *Understanding comics: The invisible art*. William Morrow.

Emiel van Miltenburg, Desmond Elliott, and Piek Vossen. 2018a. Talking about other people: an endless range of possibilities. In *Proceedings of the 11th International Conference on Natural Language Generation*, pages 415–420, Tilburg University, The Netherlands. Association for Computational Linguistics.

Emiel van Miltenburg, Ruud Koolen, and Emiel Krahmer. 2018b. Varying image description tasks: spoken versus written descriptions. In *Proceedings of the Fifth Workshop on NLP for Similar Languages, Varieties and Dialects (VarDial 2018)*, pages 88–100. Association for Computational Linguistics.

Marc Moens. 1987. Tense, aspect and temporal reference.

Jonghwan Mun, Minsu Cho, and Bohyung Han. 2017. Text-guided attention model for image captioning. In *AAAI Conference on Artificial Intelligence*.

Geoffrey K. Pullum, Rodney Huddleston, L. Bauer, B. Birner, T. Briscoe, P. Collins, D. Denison, D. Lee, A. Mittwoch, G. Nunberg, F. Palmer, J. Payne, P. Peterson, L. Stirling, and Gregory Ward. 2002. *The Cambridge Grammar of the English Language*. Cambridge University Press.

Hareesh Ravi, Lezi Wang, Carlos Muniz, Leonid Sigal, Dimitris Metaxas, and Mubbasir Kapadia. 2018. Show me a story: Towards coherent neural story illustration. In *Proceedings of the IEEE Conference on Computer Vision and Pattern Recognition*, pages 7613–7621.

Karin Kipper Schuler. 2005. Verbnet: A broad-coverage, comprehensive verb lexicon.

Piyush Sharma, Nan Ding, Sebastian Goodman, and Radu Soricut. 2018. Conceptual captions: A cleaned, hypernymed, image alt-text dataset for automatic image captioning. In *Proceedings of the 56th Annual Meeting of the Association for Computational Linguistics (Volume 1: Long Papers)*, volume 1, pages 2556–2565.

Hamed R Tavakoli, Rakshith Shetty, Ali Borji, and Jorma Laaksonen. 2017. Paying attention to descriptions generated by image captioning models. In *Proceedings of the IEEE Conference on Computer Vision and Pattern Recognition*, pages 2487–2496.

Zeno Vendler. 1957. Verbs and times. *The philosophical review*, 66(2):143–160.

Henk J Verkuyl. 2005. Aspectual composition: Surveying the ingredients. In *Perspectives on aspect*, pages 19–39. Springer.

Anthony J Viera, Joanne M Garrett, et al. 2005. Understanding interobserver agreement: the kappa statistic. *Fam Med*, 37(5):360–363.

Semih Yagcioglu, Aykut Erdem, Erkut Erdem, and Nazli Ikizler-Cinbis. 2018. Recipeqa: A challenge dataset for multimodal comprehension of cooking recipes. *arXiv preprint arXiv:1809.00812*.

Peter Young, Alice Lai, Micah Hodosh, and Julia Hockenmaier. 2014. From image descriptions to visual denotations: New similarity metrics for semantic inference over event descriptions. *Transactions of the Association for Computational Linguistics*, 2:67–78.

Learning Multilingual Word Embeddings Using Image-Text Data

Karan Singhal
Stanford University
ksinghal@cs.stanford.edu

Karthik Raman
Google AI
karthikraman@google.com

Balder ten Cate
Google AI
balder@google.com

Abstract

There has been significant interest recently in learning multilingual word embeddings – in which semantically similar words across languages have similar embeddings. State-of-the-art approaches have relied on expensive labeled data, which is unavailable for low-resource languages, or have involved post-hoc unification of monolingual embeddings. In the present paper, we investigate the efficacy of multilingual embeddings learned from weakly-supervised image-text data. In particular, we propose methods for learning multilingual embeddings using image-text data, by enforcing similarity between the representations of the image and that of the text. Our experiments reveal that even without using any expensive labeled data, a bag-of-words-based embedding model trained on image-text data achieves performance comparable to the state-of-the-art on crosslingual semantic similarity tasks.

1 Introduction

Recent advances in learning distributed representations for words (*i.e.,* word embeddings) have resulted in improvements across numerous natural language understanding tasks (Mikolov et al., 2013c; Pennington et al., 2014). These methods use unlabeled text corpora to model the semantic content of words using their co-occurring context words. Key to this is the observation that semantically similar words have similar contexts (Sahlgren, 2008), thus leading to similar word embeddings. A limitation of these word embedding approaches is that they only produce *monolingual embeddings*. This is because word co-occurrences are very likely to be limited to being within language rather than across language in text corpora. Hence semantically similar words across languages are unlikely to have similar word embeddings.

To remedy this, there has been recent work on learning *multilingual word embeddings*, in which semantically similar words within *and* across languages have similar word embeddings (Ruder, 2017). Multilingual embeddings are not just interesting as an interlingua between multiple languages; they are useful in many downstream applications. For example, one application of multilingual embeddings is to find semantically similar words and phrases across languages (Ammar et al., 2016). Another use of multilingual embeddings is in enabling zero-shot learning on unseen languages, just as monolingual word embeddings enable predictions on unseen words (Artetxe and Schwenk, 2018). In other words, a classifier using pretrained multilingual word embeddings can generalize to other languages even if training data is only in English. Interestingly, multilingual embeddings have also been shown to improve monolingual task performance (Faruqui and Dyer, 2014b; Kiela et al., 2014).

Consequently, multilingual embeddings can be very useful for low-resource languages – they allow us to overcome the scarcity of data in these languages. However, as detailed in Section 2, most work on learning multilingual word embeddings so far has heavily relied on the availability of expensive resources such as word-aligned / sentence-aligned parallel corpora or bilingual lexicons. Unfortunately, this data can be prohibitively expensive to collect for many languages. Furthermore even for languages with such data available, the coverage of the data is a limiting factor that restricts how much of the semantic space can be aligned across languages. Overcoming this data bottleneck is a key contribution of our work.

We investigate the use of cheaply available, weakly-supervised image-text data for learning multilingual embeddings. Images are a rich, language-agnostic medium that can provide a

Proceedings of the Second Workshop on Shortcomings in Vision and Language, pages 68–77
Minneapolis, USA, June 6, 2019. ©2017 Association for Computational Linguistics

bridge across languages. For example, the English word "cat" might be found on webpages containing images of cats. Similarly, the German word "katze" (meaning cat) is likely to be found on other webpages containing similar (or perhaps identical) images of cats. Thus, images can be used to learn that these words have similar semantic content. Importantly, image-text data is generally available on the internet even for low-resource languages.

As image data has proliferated on the internet, tools for understanding images have advanced considerably. Convolutional neural networks (CNNs) have achieved roughly human-level or better performance on vision tasks, particularly classification (Russakovsky et al., 2014; Szegedy et al., 2015; He et al., 2016). During classification of an image, CNNs compute intermediate outputs that have been used as generic image features that perform well across a variety of vision tasks (Sharif Razavian et al., 2014). We use these image features to enforce that words associated with similar images have similar embeddings. Since words associated with similar images are likely to have similar semantic content, even across languages, our learned embeddings capture crosslingual similarity.

There has been other recent work on reducing the amount of supervision required to learn multilingual embeddings (cf. Section 2). These methods take monolingual embeddings learned using existing methods and align them post-hoc in a shared embedding space. A limitation with post-hoc alignment of monolingual embeddings, first noticed by Duong et al. (2017), is that doing training of monolingual embeddings and alignment separately may lead to worse results than joint training of embeddings in one step. Since the monolingual embedding objective is distinct from the multilingual embedding objective, monolingual embeddings are not required to capture all information helpful for post-hoc multilingual alignment. Post-hoc alignment loses out on some information, whereas joint training does not. Duong et al. (2017) observe improved results using a joint training method compared to a similar post-hoc method. Thus, a joint training approach is desirable. To our knowledge, no previous method jointly learns multilingual word embeddings using weakly-supervised data available for low-resource languages.

To summarize: In this paper we propose an approach for learning multilingual word embeddings using image-text data jointly across all languages. We demonstrate that even a bag-of-words based embedding approach achieves performance competitive with the state-of-the-art on crosslingual semantic similarity tasks. We present experiments for understanding the effect of using pixel data as compared to co-occurrences alone. We also provide a method for training and making predictions on multilingual word embeddings even when the language of the text is unknown.

2 Related Work

Most work on producing multilingual embeddings has relied on crosslingual human-labeled data, such as bilingual lexicons (Mikolov et al., 2013b; Ammar et al., 2016; Faruqui and Dyer, 2014b; Xing et al., 2015) or parallel/aligned corpora (Klementiev et al., 2012; Ammar et al., 2016; Luong et al., 2015; Vulić and Moens, 2015). These works are also largely bilingual due to either limitations of methods or the requirement for data that exists only for a few language pairs. Bilingual embeddings are less desirable because they do not leverage the relevant resources of other languages. For example, in learning bilingual embeddings for English and French, it may be useful to leverage resources in Spanish, since French and Spanish are closely related. Bilingual embeddings are also limited in their applications to just one language pair.

For instance, Luong et al. (2015) propose BiSkip, a model that extends the skip-gram approach of Mikolov et al. (2013a) to a bilingual parallel corpus. The embedding for a word is trained to predict not only its own context, but also the contexts for corresponding words in a second corpus in a different language. Ammar et al. (2016) extend this approach further to multiple languages. This method, called MultiSkip, is compared to our methods in Section 5.

There has been some recent work on reducing the amount of human-labeled data required to learn multilingual embeddings, enabling work on low-resource languages (Smith et al., 2017; Artetxe et al., 2017; Conneau et al., 2017). These methods take monolingual embeddings learned using existing methods and align them post-hoc in a shared embedding space, exploiting the structural similarity of monolingual embedding

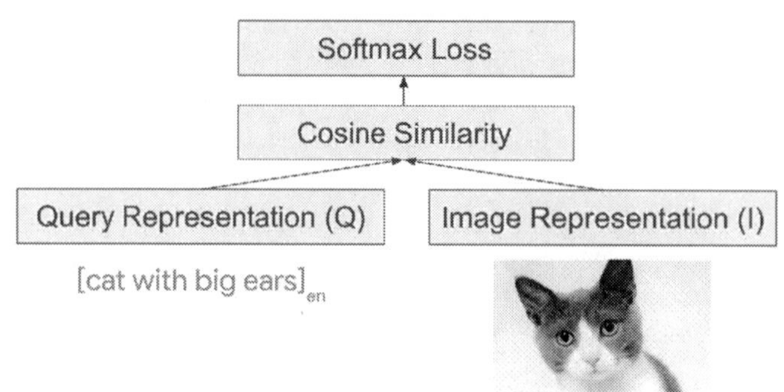

Figure 1: Our high-level approach for constraining query and image representations to be similar. The English query "cat with big ears" is mapped to Q, while the corresponding image example is mapped to I. We use the cosine similarity of these representations as input to a softmax loss function. The model task can be understood as predicting if an image is relevant to a given query.

spaces first noticed by Mikolov et al. (2013b). As discussed in Section 1, post-hoc alignment of monolingual embeddings is inherently suboptimal. For example, Smith et al. (2017) and Artetxe et al. (2017) use human-labeled data, along with shared surface forms across languages, to learn an alignment in the bilingual setting. Conneau et al. (2017) build on this for the multilingual setting, using no human-labeled data and instead using an adversarial approach to maximize alignment between monolingual embedding spaces given their structural similarities. This method (MUSE) outperforms previous approaches and represents the state-of-the-art. We compare it to our methods in Section 5.

There has been other work using image-text data to improve image and caption representations for image tasks and to learn word translations (Karpathy and Fei-Fei, 2015; Frome et al., 2013; Gella et al., 2017; Calixto et al., 2017; Hewitt et al., 2018), but no work using images to learn competitive multilingual word-level embeddings.

3 Data

We experiment using a dataset derived from Google Images search results[1]. The dataset consists of queries and the corresponding image search results. For example, one (query, image) pair might be "cat with big ears" and an image of a cat. Each (query, image) pair also has a weight corresponding to a relevance score of the image for the query. The dataset includes 3 billion (query, image, weight) triples, with 900 million

unique images and 220 million unique queries. The data was prepared by first taking the query-image set, filtering to remove any personally identifiable information and adult content, and tokenizing the remaining queries by replacing special characters with spaces and trimming extraneous whitespace. Rare tokens (those that do not appear in queries at least six times) are filtered out. Each token in each query is given a language tag based on the user-set home language of the user making the search on Google Images. For example, if the query "back pain" is made by a user with English as her home language, then the query is stored as "en:back en:pain". The dataset includes queries in about 130 languages.

Though the specific dataset we use is proprietary, Hewitt et al. (2018) have obtained a similar dataset, using the Google Images search interface, that comprises queries in 100 languages.

4 Methods

We present a series of experiments to investigate the usefulness of multimodal image-text data in learning multilingual embeddings. The crux of our method involves enforcing that for each query-image pair, the query representation (Q) is similar to the image representation (I). The query representation is a function of the word embeddings for each word in a (language-tagged) query, so enforcing this constraint on the query representation also has the effect of constraining the corresponding multilingual word embeddings.

Given some Q and some I, we enforce that the representations are similar by maximizing their cosine similarity. We use a combination of co-

---

[1] https://images.google.com

sine similarity and softmax objective to produce our loss. This high-level approach is illustrated in Figure 1. In particular, we calculate unweighted loss as follows for a query q and a corresponding image i:

$$\text{loss}(\text{Query } q, \text{Image } i) = -\log \frac{e^{\frac{Q_q^T I_i}{|Q_q||I_i|}}}{\sum_j e^{\frac{Q_q^T I_j}{|Q_q||I_j|}}}$$

where Q_q is the query representation for query q; I_i is the image representation corresponding to image i; j ranges over all images in the corpus; and $Q_q^T I_i$ is the dot product of the vectors Q_q and I_i. Note that this requires that Q_q and I_j have identical dimensionality. If a weight w is provided for the (query, image) pair, the loss is multiplied by the weight. Observe that Q and I remain unspecified for now: we detail different experiments involving different representations below.

In practice, given the size of our dataset, calculating the full denominator of the loss for a query, image pair would involve iterating through each image for each query, which is $O(n^2)$ in the number of training examples. To remedy this, we calculated the loss within each batch separately. That is, the denominator of the loss only involved summing over images in the same batch as the query. We used a batch size of 1000 for all experiments. In principle, the negative sampling approach used by Mikolov et al. (2013c) could be used instead to prevent quadratic time complexity.

We can interpret this loss function as producing a softmax classification task for queries and images: given a query, the model needs to predict the image relevant to that query. The cosine similarity between the image representation I_i and the query representation Q_q is normalized under softmax to produce a "belief" that the image i is the image relevant to the query q. This is analogous to the skip-gram model proposed by Mikolov et al. (2013a), although we use cosine similarity instead of dot product. Just as the skip-gram model ensures the embeddings of words are predictive of their contexts, our model ensures the embeddings of queries (and their constituent words) are predictive of images relevant to them.

4.1 Leveraging Image Understanding

Given the natural co-occurrence of images and text on the internet and the availability of powerful generic features, a first approach is to use generic image features as the foundation for the image representation I. We apply two fully-connected layers to learn a transformation from image features to the final representation. We can compute the image representation I_i for image i as:

$$I_i = ReLU(U * ReLU(V f_i + b_1) + b_2)$$

where f_i is a d-dimensional column vector representing generic image features for image i, V is a $m \times d$ matrix, b_1 is an m-dimensional column vector, U is a $n \times m$ matrix, and b_2 is an n-dimensional column vector. We use a rectified linear unit activation function after each fully-connected layer.

We use 64-dimensional image features derived from image-text data using an approach similar to that used by Juan et al. (2019), who train image features to discriminate between fine-grained semantic image labels. We run two experiments with m and n: in the first, $m = 200$ and $n = 100$ (producing 100-dimensional embeddings), and in the second, $m = 300$ and $n = 300$ (producing 300-dimensional embeddings).

For the query representation, we use a simple approach. The query representation is just the average of its constituent multilingual embeddings. Then, as the query representation is constrained to be similar to corresponding image representations, the multilingual embeddings (randomly initialized) are also constrained.

Note that each word in each query is prefixed with the language of the query. For example, the English query "back pain" is treated as "en:back en:pain", and the multilingual embeddings that are averaged are those for "en:back" and "en:pain". This means that words in different languages with shared surface forms are given separate embeddings. We experiment with shared embeddings for words with shared surface forms in Section 4.3.

In practice, we use a fixed multilingual vocabulary for the word embeddings, given the size of the dataset. Out-of-vocabulary words are handled by hashing them to a fixed number of embedding buckets (we use 1,000,000). That is, there are 1,000,000 embeddings for all out-of-vocabulary words, and the assignment of embedding for each word is determined by a hash function.

Our approach for leveraging image understanding is shown in Figure 2.

4.2 Co-Occurrence Only

Another approach for generating query and image representations is treating images as a black box.

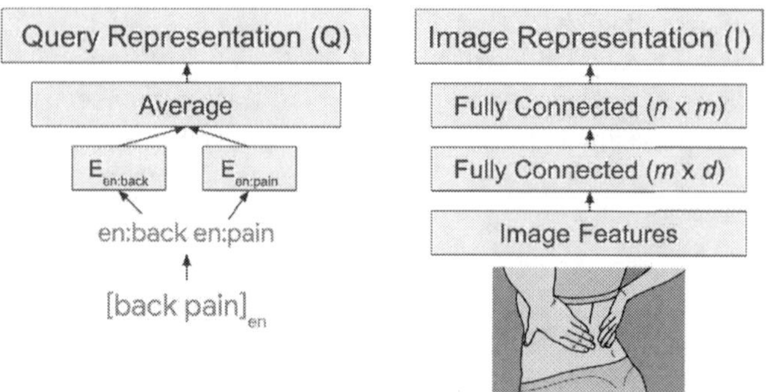

Figure 2: Our first method for calculating query and image representations, as presented in Section 4.1. To calculate the query representation, the multilingual embeddings for each language-prefixed token are averaged. To calculate the image representation, d-dimensional generic image features are passed through two fully-connected layers with m and n neurons.

Without using pixel data, how well can we do? Given the statistics of our dataset (3B query, image pairs with 220M unique queries and 900M unique images), we know that different queries co-occur with the same images. Intuitively, if a query q_1 co-occurs with many of the same images as query q_2, then q_1 and q_2 are likely to be semantically similar, regardless of the visual content of the shared images. Thus, we can use a method that uses only co-occurrence statistics to better understand how well we can capture relationships between queries. This method serves as a baseline to our initial approach leveraging image understanding.

In this setting, we keep query representations the same, and we modify image representations as follows: the image representation for an image is a randomly initialized, trainable vector (of the same dimensionality as the query representation, to ensure the cosine similarity can be calculated). The intuition for this approach is that if two queries are both associated with an image, their query representations will both be constrained to be similar to the same vector, and so the query representations themselves are constrained to be similar. This approach is a simple way to adapt our method to make use of only co-occurrence statistics.

One concern with this approach is that many queries may not have significant image co-occurrences with other queries. In particular, there are likely many images associated with only a single query. These isolated images pull query representations toward their respective random image representations (adding noise), but do not provide any information about the relationships between queries. Additionally, even for images as-sociated with multiple queries, if these queries are all within language, then they may not be very helpful for learning multilingual embeddings. Consequently, we run two experiments: one with the original dataset and one with a subset of the dataset that contains only images associated with queries in at least two different languages. This subset of the dataset has 540 million query, image pairs (down from 3 billion). For both experiments, we use $m = 200$ and $n = 100$ and produce 100-dimensional embeddings.

4.3 Language Unaware Query Representation

In Section 4.1, our method for computing query representations involved prepending language prefixes to each token, ensuring that the multilingual embedding for the English word "pain" is distinct from that for the French word "pain" (meaning bread). These query representations are *language aware*, meaning that a language tag is required for each query during both training and prediction. In the weakly-supervised setting, we may want to relax this requirement, as language-tagged data is not always readily available.

In our language unaware setting, language tags are not necessary. Each surface form in each query has a distinct embedding, and words with shared surface forms across languages (e.g., English "pain" and French "pain") have a shared embedding. In this sense, shared surface forms are used as a bridge between languages. This is illustrated in Figure 3. This may be helpful in certain cases, as for English "actor" and Spanish "actor". The image representations leverage generic

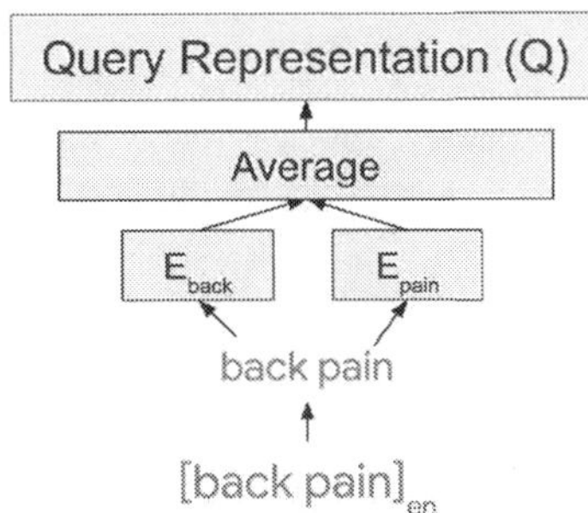

Figure 3: In our language unaware approach, language tags are not prepended to each token, so the word "pain" in English and French share an embedding.

image features, exactly as in Section 4.1. In our language-unaware experiment, we use $m = 200$ and $n = 100$ and produce 100-dimensional embeddings.

4.4 Evaluation

We evaluate our learned multilingual embeddings using six crosslingual semantic similarity tasks, two multilingual document classification tasks, and 13 monolingual semantic similarity tasks. We adapt code from Ammar et al. (2016) and Faruqui and Dyer (2014a) for evaluation.

Crosslingual Semantic Similarity This task measures how well multilingual embeddings capture semantic similarity of words, as judged by human raters. The task consists of a series of crosslingual word pairs. For each word pair in the task, human raters judge how semantically similar the words are. The model also predicts how similar the words are, using the cosine similarity between the embeddings. The score on the task is the Spearman correlation between the human ratings and the model predictions.

The specific six subtasks we use are part of the Rubenstein-Goodenough dataset (Rubenstein and Goodenough, 1965) and detailed by Ammar et al. (2016). We also include an additional task aggregating the six subtasks.

Multilingual Document Classification In this task, a classifier built on top of learned multilingual embeddings is trained on the RCV corpus of newswire text as in Klementiev et al. (2012) and Ammar et al. (2016). The corpus consists of documents in seven languages on four topics, and the classifier predicts the topic. The score on the task is test accuracy. Note that each document is monolingual, so this task measures performance within

languages for multiple languages (as opposed to crosslingual performance).

Monolingual Semantic Similarity This task is the same as the crosslingual semantic similarity task described above, but all word pairs are in English. We use this to understand how monolingual performance differs across methods. We present an average score across the 13 subtasks provided by Faruqui and Dyer (2014a).

Coverage Evaluation tasks also report a coverage, which is the fraction of the test data that a set of multilingual embeddings is able to make predictions on. This is needed because not every word in the evaluation task has a corresponding learned multilingual embedding. Thus, if coverage is low, scores are less likely to be reliable.

5 Results and Conclusions

We first present results on the crosslingual semantic similarity and multilingual document classification for our previously described experiments. We compare against the multiSkip approach by Ammar et al. (2016) and the state-of-the-art MUSE approach by Conneau et al. (2017). Results for crosslingual semantic similarity are presented in Table 1, and results for multilingual document classification are presented in Table 2.

Our experiments corresponding to Section 4.1 are titled *ImageVec 100-Dim* and *ImageVec 300-Dim* in Tables 1 and 2. Both experiments significantly outperform the multiSkip experiments in all crosslingual semantic similarity subtasks, and the 300-dimensional experiment slightly outperforms MUSE as well. Note that coverage scores are generally around 0.8 for these experiments. In multilingual document classification, MUSE achieves the best scores, and while our 300-dimensional experiment outperforms the multiSkip 40-dimensional experiment, it does not perform as well as the 512-dimensional experiment. Note that coverage scores are lower on these tasks.

One possible explanation for the difference in performance across the crosslingual semantic similarity task and multilingual document classification task is that the former measures crosslingual performance, whereas the latter measures monolingual performance in multiple languages, as described in Section 4.4. We briefly discuss further evidence that our models perform less well in the monolingual context below.

	en+es	en+de	en+fr	de+es	de+fr	fr+es	all
ImageVec 100-Dim	.75 [.87]	.77 [.87]	.84 [.74]	.80 [.83]	.76 [.77]	.77 [.73]	.79 [.81]
ImageVec 300-Dim	**.79** [.87]	.81 [.87]	**.86** [.74]	.81 [.83]	**.77** [.77]	**.80** [.73]	**.82** [.81]
ImageVec Baseline	.10 [.87]	.03 [.87]	.14 [.74]	-.25 [.83]	.07 [.77]	.15 [.73]	.08 [.81]
ImageVec Baseline 2 Lang.	.27 [.87]	.38 [.79]	.23 [.74]	.26 [.75]	.16 [.75]	.27 [.73]	.28 [.78]
ImageVec Lang. Unaware	.59 [.87]	.62 [.87]	.79 [.74]	.63 [.83]	.73 [.77]	.73 [.73]	.67 [.81]
multiSkip 40-Dim	.51 [.83]	.67 [.75]	.44 [.70]	.39 [.63]	.29 [.56]	.43 [.60]	.49 [.68]
multiSkip 512-Dim	.43 [.83]	.73 [.76]	.62 [.70]	.43 [.63]	.24 [.56]	.48 [.60]	.50 [.69]
MUSE 300-Dim	.76 [.87]	**.85** [.86]	.79 [.74]	**.83** [.81]	.73 [.77]	.74 [.73]	.79 [.80]

Table 1: Crosslingual semantic similarity scores (Spearman's ρ) across six subtasks for ImageVec (our method) and previous work. Coverage is in brackets. The last column indicates the combined score across all subtasks. Best scores on each subtask are bolded.

	en+da+it	7 Lang.
ImageVec 100-Dim	.74 [.60]	.79 [.52]
ImageVec 300-Dim	.80 [.60]	.84 [.52]
ImageVec Baseline	.60 [.60]	.59 [.52]
ImageVec Baseline 2 Lang.	.65 [.45]	.65 [.36]
ImageVec Lang. Unaware	.73 [.60]	.78 [.52]
multiSkip 40-Dim	.77 [.45]	.82 [.44]
multiSkip 512-Dim	.87 [.48]	.91 [.46]
MUSE 300-Dim	**.87** [.54]	**.91** [.51]

Table 2: Multilingual document classification accuracy scores across two subtasks for ImageVec (our method) and previous work. Coverage is in brackets. Best scores are bolded (ties broken by coverage).

Is Image Understanding Necessary? Comparing the experiments leveraging image understanding to our co-occurrence-only baseline experiments *ImageVec Baseline* and *ImageVec Baseline 2 Lang* described in Section 4.2, we see that performance is significantly degraded without pixel data (note that both experiments use 100-dimensional embeddings). Still, the results for multilingual document classification, in particular, show that we are able to learn multilingual word embeddings using co-occurrence between queries and images alone.

Interestingly, we can see that performance in the experiment in which images are filtered to be associated with at least two languages appears better than the baseline experiment on the full dataset (although coverage is low for multilingual document classification). As mentioned in Section 4.2, this may be because images without multiple queries degrade performance by introducing noise to the optimization problem. We also experimented with the same filtering on the experiments using image understanding to see if this could further boost performance (results not shown), but this reduced performance to a similar extent as random data filtering. This is likely because even isolated images (with just one query associated with an image) are still helpful for the task in this case, since the use of generic image features still constrains queries associated with similar images to have similar representations.

Even in the filtered baseline, results for both tasks are significantly lower than the methods leveraging image understanding, indicating that while co-occurrence data alone is useful, pixel data may be needed to learn competitive multilingual embeddings using our method.

Language Unaware Learning The language unaware setting only differs from the language aware one when words share a common surface form. In some cases, words sharing a common surface form have the same meaning across languages (*i.e.,* cognates). An example is "actor" in English and Spanish. In these cases, the language unaware setting may boost performance, as the embedding for "actor" effectively has more training data behind it. In other cases, words sharing a common surface form have different meanings across languages (*i.e.,* false cognates). An example is "pain" in English and French. In these cases, we expect language unawareness to reduce performance, especially if the meanings of false cognates are very different.

Our results for our 100-dimensional language unaware embeddings are presented in Tables 1 and 2 as *ImageVec Lang. Unaware*. We can see

	avg. score
ImageVec 100-Dim	.48 [.98]
ImageVec 300-Dim	.48 [.98]
ImageVec Baseline	.24 [.98]
ImageVec Baseline 2 Lang.	.33 [.95]
ImageVec Lang. Unaware	.42 [.98]
multiSkip 40-Dim	.44 [.94]
multiSkip 512-Dim	.44 [.96]
MUSE 300-Dim	**.62** [.97]

Table 3: Average monolingual semantic similarity score (Spearman's ρ) across 13 subtasks for ImageVec (our method) and previous work. Average coverage is in brackets. Best score is bolded.

that this experiment performs worse on crosslingual semantic similarity but about the same on multilingual document classification as the 100-dimensional language aware experiment (*ImageVec 100-Dim*). Still, on crosslingual semantic similarity, it significantly outperforms both multiSkip experiments. Thus, in applications where language unaware training or prediction is important, our method produces multilingual embeddings competitive with other language aware approaches.

Effect of Embedding Size In these experiments, embeddings with higher dimensionalities generally perform better in both evaluation tasks. 300-dimensional embeddings produced using our method slightly outperform 100-dimensional ones in every subtask for both tasks.

Monolingual Embedding Quality As mentioned earlier in Section 5, we suspect that the difference in performance (as compared to MUSE) on crosslingual semantic similarity and multilingual document classification for our experiments might be due to reduced monolingual performance. After all, other methods train by leveraging word contexts (and subword information, in the case of MUSE) in a large monolingual corpus, whereas we use only images as a bridge between words within and across languages. Especially for words representing abstract concepts without obvious image associations (consider the word "democracy"), it is likely that our method would produce lower quality within-language embeddings than text-only methods. This is not unexpected: Hewitt et al. (2018) found that word

translations learned via images are worse for more abstract words and Kiela et al. (2014) found that using image data is unhelpful for improving the quality of representations for some concepts.

It stands to reason then that our method would produce weaker monolingual performance. To test this, we ran 13 English monolingual semantic similarity tasks on each experiment. We present average scores in Table 3. We can see that 300-dimensional embeddings produced using our method fare significantly worse than MUSE embeddings, although they perform similarly to the multiSkip embeddings. For comparison, competitive English word embeddings achieve results similar to MUSE. This suggests that there is significant room for improvement within language (at least for English) in the quality of our learned multilingual embeddings. Improving monolingual performance would also likely boost scores across other tasks, motivating future work in this direction.

6 Discussion

We demonstrated how to learn competitive multilingual word embeddings using image-text data – which is available for low-resource languages. We have presented experiments for understanding the effect of using pixel data as compared to co-occurrences alone. We have also proposed a method for training and making predictions on multilingual word embeddings even when language tags for words are unavailable. Using a simple bag-of-words approach, we achieve performance competitive with the state-of-the-art on crosslingual semantic similarity tasks.

We have also identified a direction for future work: within language performance is weaker than the state-of-the-art, likely because our work leveraged only image-text data rather than a large monolingual corpus. Fortunately, our joint training approach provides a simple extension of our method for future work: multi-task joint training. For example, in a triple-task setting, we can simultaneously **(1)** constrain query and relevant image representations to be similar and **(2)** constrain word embeddings to be predictive of context in large monolingual corpora and **(3)** constrain representations for parallel text across languages to be similar. For the second task, implementing recent advances in producing monolingual embeddings, such as using subword information, is likely to improve results. Multilingual embeddings learned in a multi-task setting would reap both the benefits of our methods and existing methods for producing word embeddings. For example, while our method is likely to perform worse for more abstract words, when combined with existing approaches it is likely to achieve more consistent performance.

An interesting effect of our approach is that queries and images are embedded into a shared space through the query and image representations. This setup enables a range of future research directions and applications, including better image features, better monolingual text representations (especially for visual tasks), nearest-neighbor search for text or images given one modality (or both), and joint prediction using text and images.

Acknowledgments We thank Tom Duerig, Evgeniy Gabrilovich, Dan Gillick, Raphael Hoffmann, Zhen Li, Alessandro Presta, Aleksei Timofeev, Radu Soricut, and our reviewers for their insightful feedback and comments.

References

Waleed Ammar, George Mulcaire, Yulia Tsvetkov, Guillaume Lample, Chris Dyer, and Noah A. Smith. 2016. Massively multilingual word embeddings. *CoRR*, abs/1602.01925.

Mikel Artetxe, Gorka Labaka, and Eneko Agirre. 2017. Learning bilingual word embeddings with (almost) no bilingual data. In *Proceedings of the 55th Annual Meeting of the Association for Computational Linguistics (Volume 1: Long Papers)*, volume 1, pages 451–462.

Mikel Artetxe and Holger Schwenk. 2018. Massively multilingual sentence embeddings for zero-shot cross-lingual transfer and beyond. *CoRR*, abs/1812.10464.

Iacer Calixto, Qun Liu, and Nick Campbell. 2017. Multilingual multi-modal embeddings for natural language processing. *CoRR*, abs/1702.01101.

Alexis Conneau, Guillaume Lample, Marc'Aurelio Ranzato, Ludovic Denoyer, and Hervé Jégou. 2017. Word translation without parallel data. *CoRR*, abs/1710.04087.

Long Duong, Hiroshi Kanayama, Tengfei Ma, Steven Bird, and Trevor Cohn. 2017. Multilingual training of crosslingual word embeddings. In *Proceedings of the 15th Conference of the European Chapter of the Association for Computational Linguistics: Volume 1, Long Papers*, volume 1, pages 894–904.

Manaal Faruqui and Chris Dyer. 2014a. Community evaluation and exchange of word vectors at word-vectors.org. In *Proceedings of ACL: System Demonstrations*.

Manaal Faruqui and Chris Dyer. 2014b. Improving vector space word representations using multilingual correlation. In *Proceedings of the 14th Conference of the European Chapter of the Association for Computational Linguistics*, pages 462–471.

Andrea Frome, Greg S Corrado, Jon Shlens, Samy Bengio, Jeff Dean, Tomas Mikolov, et al. 2013. Devise: A deep visual-semantic embedding model. In *Advances in neural information processing systems*, pages 2121–2129.

Spandana Gella, Rico Sennrich, Frank Keller, and Mirella Lapata. 2017. Image pivoting for learning multilingual multimodal representations. *CoRR*, abs/1707.07601.

Kaiming He, Xiangyu Zhang, Shaoqing Ren, and Jian Sun. 2016. Deep residual learning for image recognition. In *Proceedings of the IEEE conference on computer vision and pattern recognition*, pages 770–778.

John Hewitt, Daphne Ippolito, Brendan Callahan, Reno Kriz, Derry Tanti Wijaya, and Chris Callison-Burch. 2018. Learning translations via images with a massively multilingual image dataset. In *Proceedings of the 56th Annual Meeting of the Association for Computational Linguistics (Volume 1: Long Papers)*, volume 1, pages 2566–2576.

Da-Cheng Juan, Chun-Ta Lu, Zhen Li, Futang Peng, Aleksei Timofeev, Yi-Ting Chen, Yaxi Gao, Tom Duerig, Andrew Tomkins, and Sujith Ravi. 2019. Graph-rise: Graph-regularized image semantic embedding. *arXiv preprint arXiv:1902.10814*.

Andrej Karpathy and Li Fei-Fei. 2015. Deep visual-semantic alignments for generating image descriptions. In *Proceedings of the IEEE conference on computer vision and pattern recognition*, pages 3128–3137.

Douwe Kiela, Felix Hill, Anna Korhonen, and Stephen Clark. 2014. Improving multi-modal representations using image dispersion: Why less is sometimes more. In *Proceedings of the 52nd Annual Meeting of the Association for Computational Linguistics (Volume 2: Short Papers)*, volume 2, pages 835–841.

Alexandre Klementiev, Ivan Titov, and Binod Bhattarai. 2012. Inducing crosslingual distributed representations of words. *Proceedings of COLING 2012*, pages 1459–1474.

Thang Luong, Hieu Pham, and Christopher D Manning. 2015. Bilingual word representations with monolingual quality in mind. In *Proceedings of the 1st Workshop on Vector Space Modeling for Natural Language Processing*, pages 151–159.

Tomas Mikolov, Kai Chen, Greg Corrado, and Jeffrey Dean. 2013a. Efficient estimation of word representations in vector space. *arXiv preprint arXiv:1301.3781*.

Tomas Mikolov, Quoc V. Le, and Ilya Sutskever. 2013b. Exploiting similarities among languages for machine translation. *CoRR*, abs/1309.4168.

Tomas Mikolov, Ilya Sutskever, Kai Chen, Greg S Corrado, and Jeff Dean. 2013c. Distributed representations of words and phrases and their compositionality. In *Advances in neural information processing systems*, pages 3111–3119.

Jeffrey Pennington, Richard Socher, and Christopher Manning. 2014. Glove: Global vectors for word representation. In *Proceedings of the 2014 conference on empirical methods in natural language processing (EMNLP)*, pages 1532–1543.

Herbert Rubenstein and John B Goodenough. 1965. Contextual correlates of synonymy. *Communications of the ACM*, 8(10):627–633.

Sebastian Ruder. 2017. A survey of cross-lingual embedding models. *CoRR*, abs/1706.04902.

Olga Russakovsky, Jia Deng, Hao Su, Jonathan Krause, Sanjeev Satheesh, Sean Ma, Zhiheng Huang, Andrej Karpathy, Aditya Khosla, Michael S. Bernstein, Alexander C. Berg, and Fei-Fei Li. 2014. Imagenet large scale visual recognition challenge. *CoRR*, abs/1409.0575.

Magnus Sahlgren. 2008. The distributional hypothesis. *Italian Journal of Disability Studies*, 20:33–53.

Ali Sharif Razavian, Hossein Azizpour, Josephine Sullivan, and Stefan Carlsson. 2014. Cnn features off-the-shelf: an astounding baseline for recognition. In *Proceedings of the IEEE conference on computer vision and pattern recognition workshops*, pages 806–813.

Samuel L Smith, David HP Turban, Steven Hamblin, and Nils Y Hammerla. 2017. Offline bilingual word vectors, orthogonal transformations and the inverted softmax. *arXiv preprint arXiv:1702.03859*.

Christian Szegedy, Wei Liu, Yangqing Jia, Pierre Sermanet, Scott Reed, Dragomir Anguelov, Dumitru Erhan, Vincent Vanhoucke, and Andrew Rabinovich. 2015. Going deeper with convolutions. In *Proceedings of the IEEE conference on computer vision and pattern recognition*, pages 1–9.

Ivan Vulić and Marie-Francine Moens. 2015. Bilingual word embeddings from non-parallel document-aligned data applied to bilingual lexicon induction. In *Proceedings of the 53rd Annual Meeting of the Association for Computational Linguistics and the 7th International Joint Conference on Natural Language Processing (Volume 2: Short Papers)*, volume 2, pages 719–725.

Chao Xing, Dong Wang, Chao Liu, and Yiye Lin. 2015. Normalized word embedding and orthogonal transform for bilingual word translation. In *Proceedings of the 2015 Conference of the North American Chapter of the Association for Computational Linguistics: Human Language Technologies*, pages 1006–1011.

Grounded Word Sense Translation

Chiraag Lala
University of Sheffield
clala1@sheffield.ac.uk

Pranava Madhyastha
Imperial College London
pranava@imperial.ac.uk

Lucia Specia
Imperial College London
l.specia@imperial.ac.uk

Abstract

Recent work on visually grounded language learning has focused on broader applications of grounded representations, such as visual question answering and multimodal machine translation. In this paper we consider grounded word sense translation, i.e. the task of correctly translating an ambiguous source word given the corresponding textual and visual context. Our main objective is to investigate the extent to which images help improve word-level (lexical) translation quality. We do so by first studying the dataset for this task to understand the scope and challenges of the task. We then explore different data settings, image features, and ways of grounding to investigate the gain from using images in each of the combinations. We find that grounding on the image is specially beneficial in weaker unidirectional recurrent translation models. We observe that adding structured image information leads to stronger gains in lexical translation accuracy.

1 Introduction

The multimodal machine translation (MMT) shared task has been conducted for the past three years (Specia et al., 2016; Elliott et al., 2017; Barrault et al., 2018) with the main goal of investigating the effectiveness of information from images in machine translation (MT). However, as acknowledged in Barrault et al. (2018), it has been difficult to evaluate the impact of multimodality (images) on the sentence-level translation quality, since the changes incurred by having an additional modality can be quite subtle. The MMT shared task consists of translating English sentences that describe an image into a target language given the English sentence itself and the image that it describes.

Recently proposed, the multimodal lexical translation (MLT) (Lala and Specia, 2018) is a

Figure 1: A labeled example from the dataset for multimodal lexical translation. Only ambiguous words in the sentence are labeled to their corresponding translation in the target language.

similar task but focused at the word level and only at ambiguous words. In MLT, the objective is to correctly translate each ambiguous word in the English source sentence into a corresponding word in the target language given the word itself, the English sentence in which it occurs and the image being described by that sentence. This is similar to the task of Visual Sense Disambiguation (Gella et al., 2016) where the objective is to disambiguate the ambiguous verbs using text and image contexts. The authors of MLT proposed to define a word in the source language to be ambiguous if it has multiple translations in the target language with different meanings in the dataset. However, they did not suggest any models for that.

In this paper, we propose to treat MLT as a sequence labeling task, as depicted by the example in Figure 1, similar to part-of-speech tagging or named entity recognition. Our approach draws inspiration from neural sequence-based approaches to word sense disambiguation (Raganato et al., 2017; Yuan et al., 2016; Kågebäck and Salomonsson, 2016) and approaches to ground machine translation (Caglayan et al., 2017). More specifically, we propose and empirically evaluate grounded translation disambiguation models based on recurrent sequential units for the task of MLT. Our primary contributions are:

- An investigation of the MLT dataset to understand the scope and challenges of the task:

Proceedings of the Second Workshop on Shortcomings in Vision and Language, pages 78–85
Minneapolis, USA, June 6, 2019. ©2017 Association for Computational Linguistics

	Train	Val	Test
Sentences	29,000	1,014	1,000
Labels EnDe	49,626	1,775	1,708
Labels EnFr	41,191	1,427	1,298

Table 1: Data splits of the dataset for multimodal lexical translation, where EnDe indicates English-German, and EnFr, English-French.

we find the task is challenging because of the skewed distribution of translation candidates in the training set and that the scope of improvements from images is about 7.8% for English-German and 8.6% for English-French.

- An investigation into data settings for the task: we find that models trained to tag all words, irrespective of their ambiguity level, perform better than other settings.

- A study on the effect of visual representations for grounded recurrent models: we find that simple unidirectional recurrent models gain more with conditioning of visual information than stronger bidirectional recurrent models.

- An investigation on different visual representations for the task: we find that structured image information (in the form of objects) perform better than the popularly used ResNet `pool5` image features.

2 Dataset for MLT

Lala and Specia (2018) extract the MLT dataset from the Multi30K (Elliott et al., 2016, 2017). MLT was also used to compute Lexical Translation Accuracy for systems submitted to the WMT18 multimodal translation shared task (Barrault et al., 2018).

The dataset consists of 31,014 images with one English description per image, where the ambiguous words in the description, if any, are labeled to their corresponding lexical translations in the target language conforming to the given context (see Figure 1). The dataset is split into training, validation and test sets in the same way as in the WMT's MMT task in 2016 (see Table 1).

2.1 Skewed Distributions of Translations

Statistics about the dataset for MLT are shown in Table 2. We emphasize that a key aspect of

Language Pair	UA	APS	APHW	TCPA	SR	WSR
EnDe	745	1.68	15.0	4.1	1.8	1.5
EnFR	661	1.39	12.5	3.0	1.6	1.3

Table 2: Some key statistics of the original dataset for MLT. UA: Unique Ambiguous words. APS: Ambiguous words Per Sentence. APHW: Ambiguous words Per Hundred Words. TCPA: Translation Candidates Per Ambiguous word. SR: Skewness Ratio as described in Section 2.1. WSR: Weigthed average of SRs.

the dataset worth noting is the skewed distribution over the lexical translation candidates. For instance, the English word *woods* has two possible lexical translations in French in this dataset - *forêt* and *bois*. Ideally, we would want both these lexical translations to occur equal number of times (uniform distribution) but in reality the distribution is skewed - *bois* occurs 79 times (we call it the Most Frequent Translation (MFT)) while *forêt* occurs 16 times.

For a better understanding of the skewness of the distributions, we define a Skewness Ratio (SR) of a word as the ratio of count of the word to the count of its most frequent translation. For example, $SR(woods) = count(woods)/count(bois) = 1.2$. For the whole dataset, we simply average the SRs over all the ambiguous words[1]. The averaged SR will be a number between 1 and the TCPA (the averaged Translation Candidates Per Ambiguous word). If it is closer to 1 this means that, in the dataset, the distribution over lexical translations is skewed. If it is closer to TCPA, then the distribution is more uniform.

We note, our definition of Skewness Ratio is similar to the inverse of 'Average Time-anchored Relative Frequency of Usage' metric defined in Ilievski et al. (2016) which is used to assess potential bias of meaning dominance with respect to its temporal popularity.

The averaged Skewness Ratios for both language pairs, mentioned in Table 2, are much closer to 1 than to their corresponding TCPAs. This implies that the distributions over the translations are highly skewed and suggests that it will be extremely challenging to demonstrate improvements over the MFT because of bias to MFT as indicated in Postma et al. (2016).

---

[1] We also compute the weighted average of SRs, called WSR in table 2, weighted by the frequency of the ambiguous word in the corpus

2.2 When Humans Find Images Useful

We extended the dataset for MLT to include the 2018 test set of MMT shared task by manually labeling the examples. In the process, human annotators were further instructed to inform whenever the image was useful in performing lexical translation.

2.2.1 Setup

The 2018 test set of the MMT shared task was made available, consisting of 1071 images and one English description per image. The ambiguous words from the original MLT dataset were searched in this test set using string matching to identify ambiguous test instances. From these test instances, the English description together with the ambiguous word and the set of all lexical translation candidates of the ambiguous word were provided to human annotators who are bilingual speakers of both English and the target language (German or French) under consideration. The corresponding images were also provided but not explicitly shown to the annotators; they had the option to look at the image if they have to and specify when they used the image.

The objective for the annotators was to select those translation candidates they thought conformed both the English description and the corresponding image; or in other words, they had to filter out the translation candidates that did not conform either the English description or the image, while having the option to look at the image (if they thought the visual context was needed to make a decision) or ignore it completely (if they thought the visual context was not needed). If they selected all available options (i.e. they did not filter out any single option) then those examples were removed from the study.

2.2.2 Results and Discussion

The human annotations of this experiment can be found together with the MLT dataset on `https://github.com/sheffieldnlp/mlt`. The results are shown in Table 3 and discussed below.

For English-German, the extension consists of 358 instances of ambiguous words. In 111 (or 31%) of these instances the annotators opted to look at the image. In 83 of these 111 image-aware instances the annotator selected the lexical translation candidate which happened to be the most frequent translation. The annotators did not know which translation candidate was the most frequent

Language Pair	Ins	Img	Img-MFT	Img-MFT / Ins (Scope)
EnDe	358	111	28	7.8%
EnFr	407	72	35	8.6%

Table 3: Results of the Human Experiment. Ins: Instances with ambiguous words. Img: the Ins instances where the Image was used. Img-MFT: the Img instances where the Most Frequent Translation was not selected (filtered out) by the annotators. Img-MFT / Ins (Scope): the ratio of Img-MFT to Ins expressed in percentage; and as discussed in Section 2.2.2 this reflects the Scope of improvement at Lexical Translation using Images.

for the given ambiguous word in the corpus. This leaves us with 28 instances, which is 7.8% of all the instances, where the annotators looked at the image and chose to filter out the most frequent translation. Although the sample size is small, these numbers help us understand the scope of image at word-level translation task (7.8% for EnDe and 8.6% for EnFr; i.e. around 8% on average).

Ambiguous words where humans opted to look at the image include *pool, hat, coat, field, wall, etc.*, suggesting textual context is not sufficient for such words. Ambiguous words where humans ignored the image include *area, fall, watch, walk, etc.*, suggesting the textual context is often sufficient to identify the correct translation.

3 Lexical Translation Models

We explore two neural sequence labeling architectures following Graves (2012), using long short-term memory networks (LSTMs)[2]:

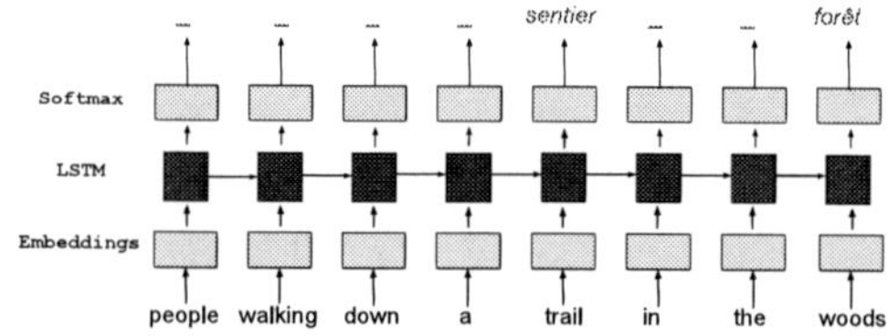

Figure 2: Unidirectional long short-term memory network used as a tagger for lexical translation of ambiguous words. The remaining unambiguous words are tagged to a common label (an underscore '_' in this case).

---

[2]We also experimented with sequence-to-sequence approaches (Sutskever et al., 2014; Cho et al., 2014; Bahdanau et al., 2015) and their application to word sense disambiguation by Raganato et al. (2017), but these performed worse.

ULSTM: This is a single layer unidirectional LSTM network (Hochreiter and Schmidhuber, 1997). A similar setting is used in Yuan et al. (2016) as a classifier for word sense disambiguation. In our setup we use the LSTM as a tagger (see Figure 2).

BLSTM: This is a single layer bidirectional LSTM network (Graves and Schmidhuber, 2005) used as a tagger. BLSTMs are used in (Kågebäck and Salomonsson, 2016) as a classifier for word sense disambiguation and have shown promising results. Recent work also suggests that BLSTM-based tagging models give state of the art performance on multilingual sequence tagging (Plank et al., 2016).

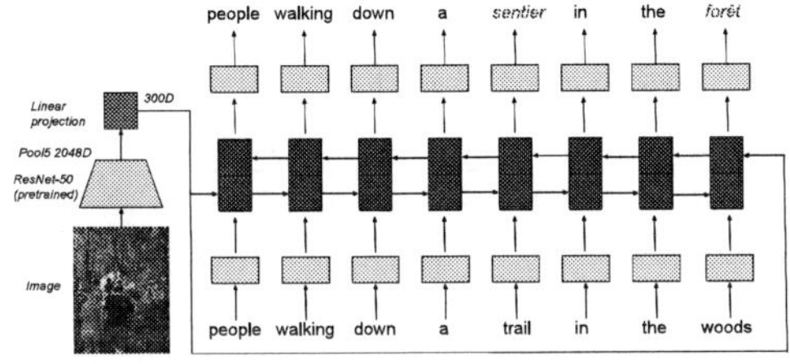

Figure 3: Multimodal-BLSTM for lexical translation of ambiguous words. Unambiguous words are tagged to self.

We extend these architectures to make them multimodal, as follows:

Multimodal Tagger: Following previous work in grounded machine translation and image captioning (Caglayan et al., 2017; Karpathy and Fei-Fei, 2015; Vinyals et al., 2015), we propose multimodal models that are identical to the text-only ULSTM and BLSTM models but are conditioned with image information. Specifically, the hidden states of the LSTMs are initialized with the image features. We used the ResNet-50 (He et al., 2016) based image features and extract 2048-dimensional features extracted from the `pool5` layer of a pre-trained ResNet-50 model. To match the dimensions of the hidden states of the LSTM, we learn a linear projection. A multimodal BLSTM architecture, trained on a data setting where we also label the unambiguous words to itself, is depicted in Figure 2.

Object-based Grounding: Given that the ambiguities are associated with content words, we assume that these correspond to objects and propose a model that uses objects in the image associated

to the ambiguous words. We experiment with two ways of incorporating object information - a) Initializing and b) Prepending.

The **Initializing** approach is identical to the multimodal tagger above where instead of the 2048-dimensional ResNet-50 image features we initialize the ULSTM and BLSTM with a binary vector representing the presence or absence of objects in the image corresponding to its ambiguous words. In the **Prepending** approach, motivated by recent work in neural machine translation (Johnson et al., 2017), we prepend the word that represents the object category (e.g. 'person') associated with the ambiguous word to the source sentence.

We extract object category information from the images using annotations on Plummer et al. (2015). These consist of a set of 16 object categories that abstractly depict the objects present in the image.

3.1 Data Settings

A significant proportion of sentences in the training (16% for EnDe and 21% for EnFr) dataset do not have any ambiguous word. Therefore at training time we experiment in two ways a) to ignore such sentences ('**ambiguous sentences**' setting); or b) train on all sentences ('**all sentences**' setting). Secondly, for unambiguous words (i.e. tokens that are not labelled), we experiment in two settings – a) leave it unlabelled ('**ambiguous word**' setting) or b) to label it to itself ('**all words**' setting). These choices amount to four different data settings for training.

3.2 Training and Baselines

Training and Evaluation: For optimization, we use the Adam (Kingma and Ba, 2014) algorithm with a learning rate = 0.001 and batch size = 32. The LSTM hidden state dimensions and the word embedding dimensions are set to 300 and the dropout rate is set to 0.3. Training is stopped early if model accuracy over the validation set does not improve for 30 epochs and then the best performing model over the validation set is selected. These models are implemented and trained in the Tensor-Flow framework.

As the focus of the task is on translating ambiguous words only, we measure the performance of all the models in terms of accuracy of correctly translating ambiguous words, ignoring the labeling accuracy on other words[3]. We also measure gains from the image, i.e. the difference (Δ) between the performance of multimodal and corresponding text-only baseline models.

Frequency Baselines: We consider baselines that completely disregard the visual and the textual contexts. The Random baseline translates an ambiguous word by selecting a translation candidate at random. The MFT baseline selects the most frequent translation of the ambiguous word as seen in the training data. As noted earlier, the most frequent translation is expected to be difficult to outperform because of the skewed distribution of translation candidates in the dataset (Postma et al., 2016).

Text-only and Image-only Baselines: The text-only baselines are the ULSTM and BLSTM that do not consider the visual contexts. The image-only baselines are the multimodal tagger conditioned on the image (either image features or object vector) except that they do not read textual context but only the ambiguous words in the sentence, i.e. all unambiguous words are removed.

4   Results and Discussion

Results of the two text-only (ULSTM and BLSTM) and two multimodal models (ULSTM+image and BLSTM+image) in the four different data settings on the test set are shown in Table 4.

We observe that all models perform better than Random baseline and most models perform better than MFT. We see that the BLSTM models always perform better than the corresponding ULSTM models, as expected.

With ResNet-50 `pool5` global image features, the multimodal ULSTM+image models perform better than the corresponding text-only ULSTM models in all data settings (See Table 4). This shows ULSTM models benefit from the ResNet-50 image features. The same cannot be said for BLSTM. Also, ULSTM tends to gain more from the image as compared to the BLSTM. We posit the lack of sufficient contextual information in ULSTMs as the reason. The visual information

---

[3] As a sanity check we note that, for all the models we experimented with, the labeling/tagging accuracy on all words (both ambiguous and unambiguous combined) ranges between 85% and 94% on the validation set and 85% and 91% on the test set.

Architectures	EnDe	Δ	EnFr	Δ
Random	24.4	-	33.6	-
MFT	65.34	-	77.73	-
all sentences + ambiguous words				
ULSTM	63.99	-	73.65	
ULSTM+image	66.10	**2.11**	75.58	**1.93**
BLSTM	67.56	-	76.89	
BLSTM+image	**68.44**	0.88	**77.66**	0.77
ambiguous sentences + ambiguous words				
ULSTM	63.58	-	74.42	
ULSTM+image	66.33	**2.75**	76.89	**2.47**
BLSTM	68.15	-	78.58	
BLSTM+image	**68.62**	0.47	**79.12**	0.54
all sentences + all words				
ULSTM	66.63	-	76.50	
ULSTM+image	66.86	**0.23**	77.12	**0.62**
BLSTM	**69.03**	-	78.35	
BLSTM+image	68.74	-0.29	**78.97**	0.62
ambiguous sentences + all words				
ULSTM	67.27	-	78.20	
ULSTM+image	67.56	**0.29**	78.27	0.07
BLSTM	69.61	-	80.35	
BLSTM+images	**69.79**	0.18	**80.43**	**0.08**

Table 4: Comparing multimodal models with their text-only counterparts in different data settings. We observe ULSTM benefits more from the ResNet-50 global image feature as compared to BLSTM.

seems to compensate for the incomplete textual context. We provide examples in Figure 4.

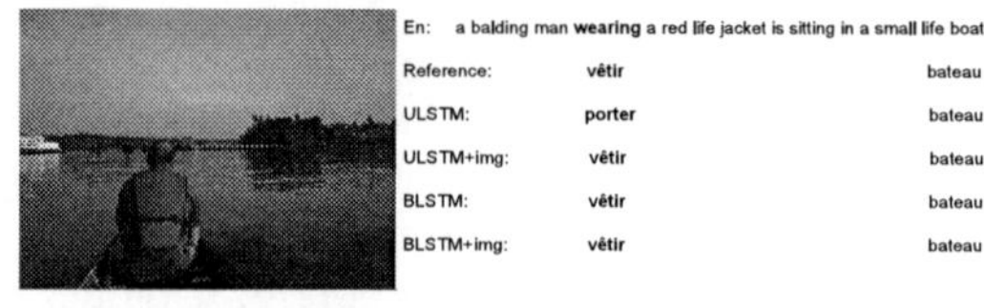

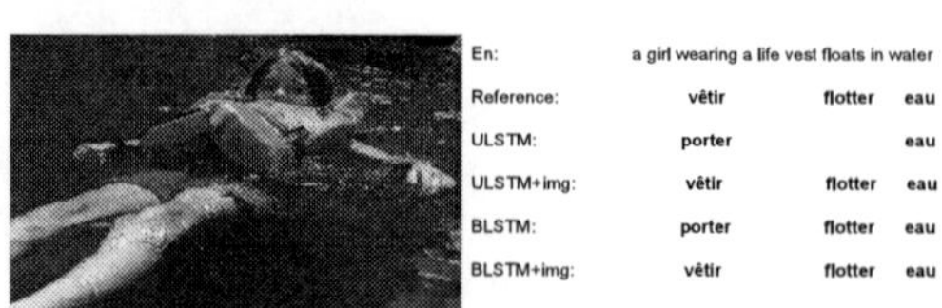

Figure 4: Examples showing ULSTM tends to benefit more from the ResNet-50 `pool5` image features as compared to BLSTM.

Further, we observe that models perform better in **all words** data settings compared to **ambiguous words** setting. This is surprising for sequence

Architectures	EnDe	Δ	EnFr	Δ
Random	24.4	-	33.6	-
MFT	65.34	-	77.73	-
all sentences + ambiguous words				
ImageOnly	67.56	-	77.20	
ObjectOnly	68.33	-	78.89	
BLSTM	67.56	-	76.89	
BLSTM+image	68.44	0.88	77.66	0.77
BLSTM+object	67.80	0.24	79.28	2.39
BLSTM+object-prepend	**70.08**	**2.52**	**80.89**	**4.00**
ambiguous sentences + ambiguous words				
ImageOnly	67.92	-	78.35	
ObjectOnly	68.15	-	79.74	
BLSTM	68.15	-	78.58	
BLSTM+image	68.62	0.47	79.12	0.54
BLSTM+object	69.03	0.88	79.43	0.85
BLSTM+object-prepend	**70.44**	**2.29**	**80.20**	**1.62**
all sentences + all words				
ImageOnly	67.56	-	77.20	
ObjectOnly	68.33	-	78.89	
BLSTM	69.03	-	78.35	
BLSTM+image	68.74	-0.29	78.97	0.62
BLSTM+object	69.85	0.82	79.89	1.54
BLSTM+object-prepend	**70.90**	**1.87**	**81.97**	**3.62**
ambiguous sentences + all words				
ImageOnly	67.92	-	78.35	
ObjectOnly	68.15	-	79.74	
BLSTM	69.61	-	80.35	
BLSTM+images	69.79	0.18	80.43	0.08
BLSTM+object	69.79	0.18	81.28	0.93
BLSTM+object-prepend	**71.02**	**1.41**	**82.59**	**2.24**

Table 5: Comparing object-based grounding BLSTM models with other BLSTM models in different data settings.

labeling since in such data settings the number of labels are larger than the source language vocabulary. Nevertheless, we observe that this data setting outperforms others. We hypothesize that a possible reason is that it forces the models to capture better context. We also note that the gains Δ from the image are larger in the **ambiguous words** data setting, especially for ULSTM. This suggests that the image information assists the model to learn better context representations. Models tend to perform slightly better in the **ambiguous sentences** setting as compared to **all sentences**. This hints that more data is not necessarily better as the unambiguous sentences are not always relevant to the task. This is in line with observations in Postma et al. (2016).

Results of our proposed object-based structured grounding models (BLSTM+object and BLSTM+objct-prepend) together with other BLSTM models are shown in Table 5. The object-based structured grounding models outperform the multimodal models that use ResNet-50 image features in most cases. More specifically, grounding via prepending performs the best in all data settings with gains over the corresponding text-only baselines ranging from 1.41% to 2.52% for EnDe and 1.62% to 4.00% for EnFr across different data settings. The best multimodal model is BLSTM+object-prepend trained in the **ambiguous sentences** and **all words** data settings and it outperforms the best performing text-only baseline model by 1.41% for EnDe and 2.24% for EnFr. This suggests that region-specific information in terms of explicit objects corresponding to the ambiguous words in the sentences are highly beneficial. We observe a similar trend when comparing the ObjectOnly baseline vs ImageOnly baseline, i.e. object information is better than ResNet-50 global image features in absence of textual context too.

5 Conclusions

We studied the MLT dataset and found that the distribution of translation candidates is very skewed making the word-level translation task challenging. In a human study, we found the scope of improvement gains from images is about 7.8% for EnDe and 8.6% for EnFr in this task on this dataset. We proposed grounded models for the task of word-level translation. We found the 'ambiguous sentences' and 'all words' data setting is most suitable for the task. Also, we found the ULSTM tends to benefit more from the image as compared to the BLSTM and posit that this is because the image compensates for the weak textual information for the ULSTM. We found that object-based grounded models, i.e. models that have explicit information about the objects associated with the ambiguities, outperform other models including ones which use the popularly used ResNet-50 `pool5` global image features. Also, we found that grounding by prepending performs better than initializing.

Acknowledgements

We thank Josiah Wang for his comments. This is supported by MultiMT (H2020 ERC Starting Grant No. 678017) and MMVC (Newton Fund Institutional Links Grant, ID: 3523433575) projects.

References

Dzmitry Bahdanau, Kyunghyun Cho, and Yoshua Bengio. 2015. Neural machine translation by jointly learning to align and translate. In *Proceedings of International Conference on Learning Representations*.

Loïc Barrault, Fethi Bougares, Lucia Specia, Chiraag Lala, Desmond Elliott, and Stella Frank. 2018. Findings of the third shared task on multimodal machine translation. In *Proceedings of the Third Conference on Machine Translation: Shared Task Papers*.

Ozan Caglayan, Walid Aransa, Adrien Bardet, Mercedes García-Martínez, Fethi Bougares, Loïc Barrault, Marc Masana, Luis Herranz, and Joost van de Weijer. 2017. LIUM-CVC submissions for WMT17 multimodal translation task. In *Proceedings of the Second Conference on Machine Translation*. Association for Computational Linguistics.

Kyunghyun Cho, Bart van Merrienboer, Caglar Gulcehre, Dzmitry Bahdanau, Fethi Bougares, Holger Schwenk, and Yoshua Bengio. 2014. Learning phrase representations using rnn encoder–decoder for statistical machine translation. In *Proceedings of the 2014 Conference on Empirical Methods in Natural Language Processing (EMNLP)*.

Desmond Elliott, Stella Frank, Loïc Barrault, Fethi Bougares, and Lucia Specia. 2017. Findings of the second shared task on multimodal machine translation and multilingual image description. In *Proceedings of the Second Conference on Machine Translation*.

Desmond Elliott, Stella Frank, Khalil Sima'an, and Lucia Specia. 2016. Multi30k: Multilingual english-german image descriptions. In *Proceedings of the 5th Workshop on Vision and Language*.

Spandana Gella, Mirella Lapata, and Frank Keller. 2016. Unsupervised visual sense disambiguation for verbs using multimodal embeddings. In *Proceedings of the 2016 Conference of the North American Chapter of the Association for Computational Linguistics: Human Language Technologies*.

Alex Graves. 2012. Supervised sequence labelling. In *Supervised sequence labelling with recurrent neural networks*. Springer.

Alex Graves and Jürgen Schmidhuber. 2005. Framewise phoneme classification with bidirectional lstm and other neural network architectures. In *Proceedings of Neural Networks*.

Kaiming He, Xiangyu Zhang, Shaoqing Ren, and Jian Sun. 2016. Deep residual learning for image recognition. In *Proceedings of the IEEE Conference on Computer Vision and Pattern Recognition*.

Sepp Hochreiter and Jürgen Schmidhuber. 1997. Long short-term memory. In *Proceedings of Neural Computation*.

Filip Ilievski, Marten Postma, and Piek Vossen. 2016. Semantic overfitting: what 'world' do we consider when evaluating disambiguation of text? In *Proceedings of COLING 2016, the 26th International Conference on Computational Linguistics: Technical Papers*.

Melvin Johnson, Mike Schuster, Quoc V Le, Maxim Krikun, Yonghui Wu, Zhifeng Chen, Nikhil Thorat, Fernanda Viégas, Martin Wattenberg, Greg Corrado, et al. 2017. Googles multilingual neural machine translation system: Enabling zero-shot translation. *Transactions of the Association for Computational Linguistics*, 5.

Mikael Kågebäck and Hans Salomonsson. 2016. Word sense disambiguation using a bidirectional lstm. In *Proceedings of International Conference on Computational Linguistics*.

Andrej Karpathy and Li Fei-Fei. 2015. Deep visual-semantic alignments for generating image descriptions. In *Proceedings of the IEEE conference on computer vision and pattern recognition*.

Diederik Kingma and Jimmy Ba. 2014. Adam: A method for stochastic optimization. In *Proceedings of International Conference on Learning Representations*.

Chiraag Lala and Lucia Specia. 2018. Multimodal lexical translation. In *Proceedings of the Eleventh International Conference on Language Resources and Evaluation (LREC 2018)*.

Barbara Plank, Anders Søgaard, and Yoav Goldberg. 2016. Multilingual part-of-speech tagging with bidirectional long short-term memory models and auxiliary loss. *The 54th Annual Meeting of the Association for Computational Linguistics*.

Bryan A Plummer, Liwei Wang, Chris M Cervantes, Juan C Caicedo, Julia Hockenmaier, and Svetlana Lazebnik. 2015. Flickr30k entities: Collecting region-to-phrase correspondences for richer image-to-sentence models. In *Proceedings of the IEEE international conference on computer vision*.

Marten Postma, Ruben Izquierdo Bevia, and Piek Vossen. 2016. More is not always better: balancing sense distributions for all-words word sense disambiguation. In *Proceedings of COLING 2016, the 26th International Conference on Computational Linguistics: Technical Papers*.

Alessandro Raganato, Claudio Delli Bovi, and Roberto Navigli. 2017. Neural sequence learning models for word sense disambiguation. In *Proceedings of the 2017 Conference on Empirical Methods in Natural Language Processing*.

Lucia Specia, Stella Frank, Khalil Sima'an, and Desmond Elliott. 2016. A shared task on multimodal machine translation and crosslingual image description. In *Proceedings of the First Conference on Machine Translation*.

Ilya Sutskever, Oriol Vinyals, and Quoc V Le. 2014.
Sequence to sequence learning with neural networks. In *Advances in Neural Information Processing Systems*.

Oriol Vinyals, Alexander Toshev, Samy Bengio, and
Dumitru Erhan. 2015. Show and tell: A neural image caption generator. In *Proceedings of the IEEE
conference on computer vision and pattern recognition*.

Dayu Yuan, Julian Richardson, Ryan Doherty, Colin
Evans, and Eric Altendorf. 2016. Semi-supervised
word sense disambiguation with neural models. In
*Proceedings of the 26th International Conference on
Computational Linguistics: Technical Papers*.

Author Index

Alikhani, Malihe, 58
Androutsopoulos, Ion, 26

Belinkov, Yonatan, 1

Conser, Erik, 37

Davis, Larry, 14

Grand, Gabriel, 1

Hahn, Kennedy, 37

Kougia, Vasiliki, 26

Lala, Chiraag, 78

Madhyastha, Pranava, 78
Mitchell, Melanie, 37
Modi, Yatri, 47
Morariu, Vlad, 14

Parde, Natalie, 47
Pavlopoulos, John, 26

Raman, Karthik, 68

Shrivastava, Abhinav, 14
Singhal, Karan, 68
Specia, Lucia, 78
Stone, Matthew, 58

ten Cate, Balder, 68

Watson, Chandler, 37
Wiriyathammabhum, Peratham, 14